P9-CBM-658

KAPLAN

Other Kaplan Books to Help You Prepare For Your Future

The Buck Starts Here: The Beginner's Guide to Smart Financial Choices
Going Indie: Self-Employment, Freelance, & Temping Opportunities
Kaplan/Newsweek Business School Admissions Adviser
Kaplan/Newsweek Graduate School Admissions Adviser
Kaplan/Newsweek Law School Admissions Adviser
Kaplan/Newsweek Medical School Admissions Adviser
Reality 101
Résumé Builder & Career Counselor
The Yale Daily News Guide to Internships
The Yale Daily News Guide to Fellowships and Grants

CARNEGIE LIBRARY
_IVINGSTONE COLLEGE
SALISBURY, NC 28144

STUDENT'S GUIDE TO ON-CAMPUS JOB RECRUITMENT

by Elizabeth Phythian

Kaplan Books
Published by Kaplan Educational Centers and Simon & Schuster
1230 Avenue of the Americas
New York, NY 10020

Copyright © 1998, by Kaplan Educational Centers. All rights reserved.

No part of this book may be reproduced or transmitted in any form or by any means, electronic or mechanical, including photocopying, recording, or by any information storage and retrieval system, without the written permission of the Publisher, except where permitted by law.

For bulk sales to schools, colleges, and universities, please contact Renee Memi, Simon & Schuster Special Markets, 1633 Broadway, 8th Floor, New York, NY 10019.

Kaplan® is a registered trademark of Kaplan Educational Centers.

Project Editor: Julie Schmidt
Cover Design: Cheung Tai
Production Editor: Maude Spekes
Desktop Publishing Manager: Michael Shevlin
Managing Editor: Brent Gallenberger
Executive Editor: Del Franz

Special thanks to: Gerard Capistrano, Richard Christiano, Evelyn Lontok, Kiernan McGuire, Joyce Smith, and Linda Volpano

Manufactured in the United States of America
Published simultaneously in Canada

August 1998

10 9 8 7 6 5 4 3 2 1

Library of Congress Cataloguing-in-Publication Data
Phythian, Elizabeth.
    Student's guide to on-campus job recruitment/ by Elizabeth Phythian.
        p.   cm.
    ISBN 0-684-85238-1
    1. Job hunting. 2. College graduates—Employment. 3. Students—
    Employment. I. Title.
    HF5382.P48   1998
    650.14—dc21   98-15110
                                                              CIP

ISBN: 0-684-85238-1

CONTENTS

ABOUT THE AUTHOR

Elizabeth (Liz) Phythian was one of the original employees of *SCORE!* Educational Centers, a provider of after-school enrichment programs for elementary and middle school students. Liz held a variety of positions while working at *SCORE!*, including that of recruiting director. In this capacity, Liz personally interviewed over 700 candidates, reviewed thousands of résumés, and devoted considerable time and effort to the recruiting process.

A native of the San Francisco Bay Area, Liz received her undergraduate degree in English from Columbia University and her master's in English from the University of Virginia.

DEDICATION

For my parents who always believed I could get the job done, and for Alan and Rob for giving me the chance.

—Elizabeth Phythian

INTRODUCTION

Timing is everything. Only a few short years ago, employment prospects for college graduates were bleak. This year, with the economy booming and unemployment at its lowest point since the late 1980's, the job outlook is the brightest in years.

—Penny Singer, "A Bright Job Outlook for the Class of '97," *The New York Times*, 22 June, 1997.

Unless you've been living under a rock, you may have heard something about these hiring trends on campus. Check out any paper, from the *Wall Street Journal* to the *Washington Post*. You'll find numerous articles on the increased interest that a variety of companies, from investment banks to software developers, are showing in college graduates. At some schools, the demand for college graduates is greater than the career centers can accommodate. In 1997, UCLA's Career Center had a waiting list of 150 companies wanting to recruit on campus, according to the *Wall Street Journal*.

What exactly is "on-campus recruiting"? At the beginning of every school year, companies arrange to visit college campuses for the purpose of recruiting graduating seniors to work for them. A company's on-campus recruiting activities might include on-campus interviewing, career fair participation, information session presentations, career workshops, mock interviews, or panel discussions.

The economic outlook for the year affects the number of organizations participating in on-campus recruiting. William Currin, the Director of the Office of Career Services at Wake Forest University, claimed in an article published by *Triad Business News* that the "1996–1997 recruiting season was the best he has seen at Wake in more than 10 years," reflecting the healthy state of the American economy. Whether or not a company chooses to participate will also depend on factors such as the size of the student body, geographic location, and the academic reputation of the school. The size of the company and whether it is in a hiring freeze or a growth spurt will also affect its efforts on campus.

On-campus recruiting gives companies a relatively easy way to tap into a strong pool of potential new employees while providing students with unusual opportunities to find jobs. Yet many students seem to stumble upon the career center and on-campus recruiting activities too late in the year to take full advantage of the tremendous resources available to them.

This book draws on the experience of professional on-campus recruiters to offer a perspective on on-campus recruiting from "the other side of the table." It's full of practical guidelines for students who want to navigate the on-campus recruiting process successfully. If you're such a student, you'll find insights on how you should comport yourself in researching, applying for, and interviewing for jobs, as well as pointers on how to negotiate a good job offer. You'll get advance warning of common mistakes that college students make, and advice in anticipating what companies want from you.

If you're a typical college student, you're juggling details—figuring out how you can maximize your college years before you hit that so-called real world. You're busy. But you're also in a unique position to talk to prospective employers, a position that many students don't appreciate or bother to explore until it's too late. Of course, the job market doesn't disappear once you're out of school. But a job search is like so many other challenges you face as a student—the more you put into it, the more you get out of it. If you can get your act together a little earlier, you'll benefit enormously by taking advantage of the companies that are not only willing but perhaps eager to hire you.

Take a deep breath, close your eyes, and exhale slowly. Savor this moment. You're about to experience one of the only times in your job-hunting career when employers come to you instead of the other way around. Granted, the field can be competitive. If you've sought out internship or work experience, participated in extracurricular activities, or performed well academically, you'll have a better shot than others. But even if you haven't done all these things, you'll benefit from the fact that college graduates are facing one of the best job markets for entry-level employment in years. Why not make the most of it?

section **1**

GETTING STARTED

1

ON-CAMPUS RECRUITMENT

WHAT IS ON-CAMPUS RECRUITMENT?

From the beginning of autumn classes to the end of spring term, companies actively recruit college seniors through participation in career fairs, information sessions, other events, and, most importantly of all, on-campus interviews. Most of these events are designed to help spread the word to students about a particular company and the opportunities that are available at that company. In effect, companies are marketing themselves to you, sometimes with carefully orchestrated campaigns.

Career Fairs

Career fairs are school-sponsored events attended by companies that pay for the privilege of bringing representatives and literature on campus. Company representatives mingle with students and talk up opportunities. Students attend career fairs to gauge which companies are hiring in an informal, convenient setting.

If you've ever come across a group of people in a crowded auditorium or plaza, milling about in everything from power suits to tie dyes, you've seen a career fair. It's sometimes difficult to tell the student from the recruiter, as more and more companies opt for khakis

Go for the Goodies

Forget the jobs for a minute. Go to a career fair and you just might come home with:

Tote bags

Water bottles

Coffee mugs

Stress balls

Sparkly pencils

Glittery key chains

Candy

and a company polo shirt, while students occasionally wear their best pinstripes. What you wear isn't as important as showing up. This is your chance to get a taste of the company culture, to pick up recruiting literature, to impress a recruiter, or to discover an interesting opportunity.

You'll usually find all of the companies slated to interview on campus, plus quite a few others, at the career fair. These companies represent a wide range of industries. When you arrive at the fair, you'll probably be given a map and a program of those attending. Most career centers will group attending companies by an industry category (finance, education, nonprofits, etcetera), while others will alphabetize the participants.

Tough to Categorize

Many companies are tough to categorize. If you limit yourself to exploring only those listed under your industry choice, you may miss out on good opportunities listed under other categories. Look at the company descriptions to learn more about who is attending a career fair. For example, the company *SCORE!* Educational Centers is technically educational, but it also offers jobs in the areas of marketing, management, and small business.

Career fairs take place at different times during the year, depending on the host school. Often held towards the beginning of the term, they can be sponsored by the career center or by a student group (such as an undergraduate business fraternity). Some schools hold only one fair per academic year. These fairs usually last one day and run from late morning to early afternoon.

If you attend a school that's either too small or too remote to hold a career fair, ask your career center about career consortiums. These are joint career fairs held by groups of schools, often small liberal arts colleges that don't have a large enough student population to attract company recruiters on their own.

Information Sessions

Information sessions are informal presentations in which representatives from a company speak to a group of students on campus. The idea behind the info session is that recruiters save time by presenting info on job descriptions, company growth, mission statements, and company culture to a group rather than to individuals. You may see slide-show presentations, overheadprojector slides, a panel discussion, a video tape, or a one-person show. Info sessions also serve as opportunities for companies to sell potential employees on the benefits of working with them. Finally, an info session is a chance for employers to check out who is interested in interviewing with them and to screen a little before interviewing on-campus.

Info sessions are held at the career center, in the student union, in the faculty house, or at a nearby hotel. As with the career fair, attire can vary. You'll probably want to bring a résumé as well as some questions, as this is often an interactive evening. In most cases, information sessions are open to anyone. Some companies will limit attendance or issue invitations to students who meet certain requirements, such as majoring in a particular subject.

For Minority and Female Applicants Only

Crimson & Brown specializes in the recruitment of top minority and women candidates for a variety of firms. This organization sets up large career forums, annual events that take place between November and January and offer interviews and career fairs. If you attend school outside of Boston, New York, Washington, D.C., Chicago, or San Francisco, this could be a nice resource for you. More information is available at the Crimson & Brown Web site at http://www.cbacareers.com.

Other Events

Company recruiters are often encouraged to come on campus and hold *"mock" interviews*, short sessions that give students the chance to practice interviewing skills while learning more about certain career fields. This is a great chance for you to check out which companies are most actively participating in recruiting on campus, as well as to practice essential question-asking and -answering skills.

Some career centers also schedule *lecture series* in which authorities come in and speak to groups of students. A company representative might come in to address topics ranging from professional development to changing technology applications. More often than not, these are held as panel discussions, particularly if a career center is sponsoring an event such as: "Majoring in History? Some Possible Career Choices for the History Major."

The competition for top graduates is increasing. Some companies have reached the conclusion that career fairs, info sessions, mock interviews, lecture series, and on-campus interviewing no longer suffice as recruitment tactics. The *Wall Street Journal* reported that companies are increasingly taking less conventional approaches to recruitment, going so far as to bring plastic mountains or holographs to campus or to give away water guns or Frisbees.

On-Campus Interviewing

What does all of this activity lead up to? An interview. On-campus interviews are prescheduled meetings between a student candidate and a company representative—often a full-time recruiter, a manager responsible for the job being filled, or an employee who is an alumnus of your school. These interviews are scheduled through career centers, and may be obtained through employer preselection, bidding, or open schedules (see chapter 5 for a detailed description of these options)

On-campus interviews usually run for half an hour, although companies may opt for 45- or even 60-minute interview schedules. Most often you will meet with one representative of the company; on occasion, you'll meet with two or even three representatives. Some companies will reserve two interview rooms and, if you seem like an especially strong candidate, will invite you to remain longer than your scheduled time to meet with another representative.

WHO SHOULD PARTICIPATE?

For a variety of reasons, you may be under the impression that participating in career fairs, info sessions, and on-campus interviews would be a waste of time for you. Let's take a moment to clear up a few common misconceptions that students have about on-campus recruitment.

(1) "On-campus interviewing is only for 'wannabe' bankers or accountants—why should I bother with the power suits when I don't want that kind of job?"

Traditionally, it is true, on-campus recruiting has been confined to the finance industry, especially accounting, banking, and consulting (such as Deloitte & Touche, J. P. Morgan, or Andersen Consulting). This is no longer the case. During any given recruiting season, you might also see companies from these fields:

- Retail management (e.g., J. Crew, and May Department Stores)
- Education (public and private schools, and a growing number of education-oriented service providers like Kaplan Educational Centers, *SCORE!* Educational Centers, and Princeton Review)
- Nonprofit organizations (e.g., Teach for America, the Peace Corps, Summerbridge, and Americorps)
- Government agencies and armed services (e.g., the Secret Service and the Navy)
- National sports organizations (e.g., the NBA)
- High tech firms (e.g., Oracle, Sun Microsystems, and Microsoft)
- Advertising, P.R., and marketing companies (e.g., Ogilvy & Mather, sports marketers, and Internet marketers)

During the '97–'98 school year at Northwestern University, over 180 companies representing many industries participated in on-campus interviews. And University of Virginia expected more than 450 companies (from big business, regional business, and the federal government) to hold on-campus interviews.

(2) "I'm an American Studies major. Nobody would want to hire me because I don't have any 'practical' skills."

Don't despair if you haven't chosen a "practical" major like business or computer engineering. Although this might limit you somewhat in terms of the opportunities available to you, in general, companies are less interested in what you are studying than in what you have learned. An individual who has strong communication, academic, problem-solving, analytical, writing, and/or public speaking skills—regardless of his or her major—could well be a strong contender for a wide variety of jobs.

The point being made is that whatever your major or career interest, you'll need to plan ahead for graduation. We strongly encourage you to at least visit the career center to see what services are available, and to do so early on in your college career. The amount of time required to attend some info sessions, wander through a few career fairs, or check out the career forums offered is pretty minor, considering what you could gain.

(3) "Companies only come on campus in the first few months of the year. What if I don't know what field I want to go into? I can't possibly get my act or my résumé together that quickly!"

The earlier you start, obviously, the more options you will have. But don't just give up by the time Halloween rolls around. Some companies will continue to visit campuses in the winter and spring terms. There is a strong chance that hopeful employers will be interviewing into the spring, sometimes as late as May.

(4) "I live 1,500 miles from school and I'm planning on going home after graduation. Wouldn't it be a waste of time for me to go through on-campus interviews, since I won't even be in the area?"

While certain smaller, local companies look for employees in the vicinity of your school, many larger or expanding organizations hire for more than one region. Always check out the options before deciding whether to go through on-campus interviews or to focus your job search on your hometown. Clearly, if you live in Anchorage, Alaska, but attend college in Minnesota, it will be harder to find employment than if you hailed from a booming town in the south like Atlanta, Georgia. If you're willing to relocate, of course, on-campus interviewing is an opportunity you should definitely not pass up.

Now that you have an idea of some of the ways companies publicize opportunities and how on-campus interviews work, you'll need to get started on your job search. To find out specifics on who is participating in recruiting at your school and to get important dates for career fairs, info sessions, and interviewing deadlines, you can read company ads in your school newspaper. These ads often provide dates as well as company contacts. An even better way to learn about events is to go directly to the source. It's time to go to your career center.

chapter 2

THE CAREER CENTER

Often called the Career Center, Career Services, or Career Planning Center, the size and the services offered by your school's career center depend on your college's location, enrollment, endowment, and academic reputation, among other things. Ask somebody to give you a tour of the center and a rundown of the services available. Career centers handle all of the scheduling and the logistics for on-campus interviewing. Your career center may also offer counseling services, résumé-writing and interviewing guidance, career programming, and a library of useful job-hunting tools and resources.

REGISTERING

The registration process is simple enough. Some schools will even let you do this online. In general, you don't need to participate in on-campus interviewing to have access to other resources at the career center, but you will need to register to interview with companies on campus and, in some cases, to use the center.

CAREER COUNSELORS

Check out your school's counseling facilities. Career counselors may be able to administer and help you to interpret the results of skills-assessment or inventory tests such as the computer-based DISCOVER or SIGI (System for Interactive Guidance and Information). Counselors often belong to profes-

Visit Online

If you're feeling a bit gun-shy about showing up at the career center with no preparation, try visiting your career center online. Go to your school's Web site. The link to the career center is usually listed under "Jobs," "Careers," or "Employment Information."

sional associations such as the National Association of Colleges and Employers (NACE). They have access to company presentations, panel discussions, and other "inside" information on company hiring trends, as well as statistics on how alumni have fared on the job market in previous years. They know all about career workshop schedules and any other services available in the center. It's important to remember, however, that while counselors are available to provide you with guidance, they are not there to make decisions for you.

THE CAREER CENTER LIBRARY

Library resources—like everything else—vary by school. Here's a list of the kinds of things you might find in the career center library.

Alumni Database

This could include contact names for informational interviews, possible internship sources, or alumni representatives from companies that are actively recruiting on campus.

Books

You'll find books on almost every aspect of the job hunt, including how to write a résumé or cover letter, tips on landing an interview, practice interview questions, and breakdowns of companies by industry.

Career Fields Information

At the very least, the library should have a recent copy of the *Occupational Outlook Handbook*, published by the Department of Labor's Bureau of Labor Statistics. It includes job descriptions, career outlook forecasts, and salary info for an array of industries.

Case Study Examples

Certain kinds of companies, particularly consulting firms, like to give you a case study as part of your interview. Your career center should have examples on file that students may use for practice.

Company Binders or Brochure Library

When companies list job opportunities or plan to interview students on campus, they often send a binder of company literature with job descriptions, financial information, and, perhaps, a stack of brochures that students may take home. Check with your career center on whether or not you may remove information. Some things are meant to remain in the library.

Occupational Files

Sometimes as simple as a collection of recent news clippings, these files can cover everything from general company backgrounds to salary ranges for alumni who went into a certain field.

Practice Interviews

See if your career center offers students the chance to practice interviewing. Look for a collection of videos that you can watch to learn more about interview skills and opportunities to interview with a career center staffperson or participate in "mock" interviews with company representatives coming on campus.

Recruiting Literature Databases

Some career centers have databases of company recruiting literature that you can search by key word, employer name, type of business, or location.

Sample Applications

Because some companies will ask you to fill out application forms, career centers sometimes keep examples on file for you to examine.

World Wide Web Access

This is especially helpful when looking up companies' Web sites or other online job listings.

INTERNSHIP PROGRAMS

Many companies—especially the larger ones—have well-established internship programs that provide undergraduates with the chance to prove themselves before actually going on the market for a full-time job. Some career centers will carry recent editions of books listing national internship opportunities (often broken down by location as well as by industry). You may also find an internship database, alumni contacts at companies with established internship programs, or binders of internship opportunities. Some schools sponsor career fairs in the winter or early spring that are specifically for internships.

JOB LISTINGS

Career centers maintain databases or binders of current, full-time job listings. These fall into two categories: immediate and future openings. While companies generally use on-campus interviews to hire people who will start work sometime after commencement, they have the opportunity to list immediate openings with career centers as well. The immediate openings are directed more towards alumni or mid-year graduates; still, it's a good idea to scan these job listings and become familiar with the job titles and job descriptions within the field of your interest, not to mention salary ranges and opportunities for advancement. If you've done your research here, you'll be that much better prepared in the event that you land an interview.

Search from Afar

If you're looking for employment in an area other than where you attend school, you may want to check the job listings binder or database on a regular basis. Some centers separate out-of-state from local opportunities for you. Companies that are interested in hiring alumni from your school and that are unable to come out for interviews may list their opportunities in the job listings binder. While you won't be able to interview with the company face-to-face on campus, you'll at least know who's hiring.

Access to JOBTRAK

The internet is rapidly becoming an effective job-hunting tool. Most college career centers now work with

Jobtrak, an online listing service that receives job listings from companies, formats them, and makes them available online for students and alumni of the schools specified by the company listing the job. Career centers either provide students online access to Jobtrak listings or print these listings out and keep them in binders.

You have the option of logging on to Jobtrak's Web page at http://www.jobtrak.com and browsing through any listings on your own, as long as you have your career center's password. These listings are updated daily and include both full-time and part-time opportunities. You may search by occupation, location, or key words. If you're interested in looking for work in another part of the country, you can quickly access listings there. Jobtrak also features a "Top Recruiters" section and links to some company websites.

NEWSLETTER

Many centers put together a newsletter that comes out anywhere from one to four times a month. The newsletter is a great source of updates on upcoming info sessions, additions to the companies interviewing on campus, unusual job listings, and center career programming. It is sometimes available online.

Now that you have a good idea of the types of resources available at your career center, it's time to plan your job search.

chapter 3
MANAGING YOUR SEARCH

WHY YOU NEED A PLAN

Let's say you've got a paper to do. It's been on the syllabus all term, looming on your horizon each time you blow off homework to go to the movies. If procrastination is an art, you must be a master. Sound familiar? It should. Most of us can't stand the thought of starting something weeks in advance, allowing ourselves a bit of time every day to lessen the burden as deadlines draw near.

Think of your job search as the ultimate research paper, requiring forethought, planning, and some revision. You're much better prepared for this task than you might think. You have three major reasons for approaching the job search with confidence:

1. Research Skills

You've developed the ability to research a subject thoroughly. We're suggesting that you apply those skills to an assignment that won't be graded or assigned by anyone but you.

2. Contacts

These may include friends, alumni, professors, parents, parents' friends, or friends' parents . . . be aware that anyone and everyone you know knows someone who's working in the "real world."

3. Resources

Libraries, Internet access, computer labs, career centers, department resources, and academic and/or student advisors are all resources that you should exploit in your job search.

You have obstacles as well, in the form of exams, classes, and all of the deadlines that accompany a full load of courses. Not to mention the social obligations of being a student. But answer this: What's ultimately going to be more important? The extra two hours studying for the calculus final, or two hours finding out which companies will be recruiting on campus this spring? There's an old adage about not seeing the forest for the trees. As a college student, you'll want to pay attention to the trees. But never lose sight of the forest.

Phases of the Job Search

- Assessing what you're good at, enjoy doing, and are interested in

- Researching which companies or fields will provide a career that fits your interests

- Narrowing the field to a reasonable number of companies to research, contact, and interview with

- Putting an application together, including a résumé and cover letter that's written with your target company or career in mind

- Setting up interviews and preparing for them

- Deciding on your options

How you go about tackling these phases is up to you. However, giving yourself a schedule, complete with deadlines, is an important step in managing a job search while continuing to do well in school. You might even allot a certain amount of time to spend looking for a job each week to ensure that you spread out the work over a longer period of time.

To embark upon a research project of this nature, you need the correct tools. You'll want to find a good calendar to note down deadlines and events. It would be a good idea to get files, index cards, and devise a filing system to help you keep track of company contacts. If you're willing to sit down and set some goals and work within deadlines, you'll save yourself headaches later on. Finding a job is a combination of planning, hard work, persistence, and follow-through, as well as a little luck.

A SAMPLE CHECKLIST

Your school's career center may have some helpful information to give you about where you should be in your search. Take a look at the following sample checklist, which is adapted from Northwestern University Career Services' Career Planning Process Timeline:

The Career Planning Process

Start planning in your freshman year, and intensify your preparations as you get closer to graduating.

Freshman Year

- Begin the self-assessment process. Consider your interests, values, skills, and motivations.
- Become familiar with career and employment resources on the Internet through your career center's home page.
- Start to explore various careers. Acquaint yourself with the materials in the Career Center library.
- Develop a tentative career development plan.
- Formulate a skill development plan.
- Visit the Student Employment Office to explore part-time and summer jobs, internships, or to investigate volunteer opportunities that could provide you with exposure to work settings and job functions that could be useful to you in the future.
- Identify and participate in campus and community activities.

Sophomore Year

- Become involved in student organizations, volunteer work, and/or part-time employment to develop new skills and interests.
- Meet with a career counselor to discuss your skills, values, and interests, and relate this to your choice of a major and future career options.
- Choose and declare your major and plan your curriculum with the assistance of an academic adviser.

- Investigate internship, externship, or co-op opportunities through academic offices and your school's student employment program.
- Investigate off-campus study or independent research in your chosen academic field.
- Begin to attend career information seminars and employer presentations.
- Explore the academic and practical-experiential requirements for entering the profession of your choice.
- Develop associations with faculty members, administrators, and career counselors.
- Write a résumé.
- Obtain a summer job or internship related to your potential field of interest.

Junior Year

- Select elective courses that will broaden your academic foundation and expand your employment opportunities.
- Join campus and community organizations to develop your leadership and teamwork skills.
- Begin the decision-making process to determine if you want to attend graduate school or pursue employment.
- Narrow career alternatives, using the DISCOVER computerized career-planning system, and meet with a career counselor who can assist you in the career decision-making process.
- Research key organizations, industries, corporations, and businesses through resources in the career center library.
- Conduct informational interviews and use the alumni network.
- Obtain a career-related internship and reality-test your values, skills, and interests.

Senior Year

- Register with the Placement Center and attend orientation sessions. Get your résumé approved.
- Organize your job search early.
- Identify necessary steps and develop an implementation plan.

- Attend career development, interviewing, and job-search workshops.
- Use the career center library to identify employment opportunities, company literature, and salary information.
- Register for on-campus interviewing.
- Review job listings on the Internet.

Are you panicking as you read this because you're a senior who has yet to set foot in the career center? If so, calm down—you still have time. It's true that for the truly enterprising student, visiting the career center and taking advantage of the various career fairs on campus as a freshman is a great idea. The sooner you get started, the better, but it's never too late to start exploring your options. The process might also start two weeks into the first quarter of your senior year or, more realistically, after you finish exams and have some time over winter break to examine your future. While five months before graduation doesn't give you much time, it will suffice if you use it well.

On-campus recruiting opportunities may be available as late as May in the spring term of your senior year. If you manage to get your act together only after you graduate, keep in mind that some schools will allow recent graduates to participate in on-campus interviews, although they may demand a small fee for this service. Even if you start your search after all the deadlines have passed and miss the chance to interview, you can still benefit from the other services the career center provides.

Don't expect to find a great job overnight. Not only is it likely to take time for you to locate good opportunities, you'll also have to put some effort into presenting yourself in the best possible manner to the companies with which you eventually interview. The next chapter will provide you with some useful tips on how to put an impressive job application together.

chapter 4
PUTTING YOUR APPLICATION TOGETHER

RÉSUMÉS

A résumé is a piece of blank paper that should be filled with academic, work, and activity experiences that convey a sense of your skills and potential. It's a difficult but essential part of your job application.

Your career center will have books, brochures, examples and, perhaps, a counselor who will review your résumé and approve it before you send it anywhere. Some centers can even give you a résumé template on disk. Yet despite all the help that is available, students persist in making major errors on their résumés. Here's a short list of mistakes recruiters see all too often.

THE TOP 13 MISTAKES STUDENTS MAKE ON THEIR RÉSUMÉS:

1. Typos
Do *not* rely on spell checkers to catch mistakes. Double check every part of your address as well—you'd be amazed at how many people reverse digits in their phone numbers or zip codes!

2. Grammatical Errors
Just because everything is spelled correctly doesn't mean that everything is used correctly. A frightening number of college seniors use "their" instead of "there," "it's" instead of "its," and "you're" instead of "your." If you're not absolutely positive you're using something correctly, look it up!

3. Holes in the Résumé

Are there gaps in your employment or academic history? Did you take a term off or spend two years overseas without explaining it on your résumé? Employers will want a clear picture of what you've done during your summers and which jobs you've held during the school year. There are ways to account for trips abroad or for taking a break from school.

4. Inconsistent Formatting

Did you bold one header but forget to do another? Do all of your tabs line up? Did you capitalize all of your headers but one? It may sound nit-picky, but employers look at your résumé as a writing sample that you've had time to polish, proofread, and look over. It should be flawless.

5. Two-page Résumés

Unless you've been in your field for ten years, have held numerous jobs, received many awards, and/or published some papers, keep your résumé to one page.

6. Lying

No matter how small the embellishment, it's not okay. Don't add a few months to your tenure with a company, up your GPA by two-tenths of a point, or make up leadership experience that never happened. Anything you put down is fair game for an employer to check. If you're tempted to pad your experience, don't. It's a dumb idea.

7. Microscopic Type Fonts and Margins

Avoid small type. It's acceptable to change margins a bit to accommodate text, but don't make them too narrow. Margins are there for a reason.

8. Too Much Text

Leave as much white space as possible, while giving a reasonable amount of information about the job. Don't write a prose résumé with huge paragraphs of text. It should be easy to read.

9. Death by Overdose

Don't get caught up in so much fancy formatting that your résumé becomes a work of art that can't be read. Lovely, colorful fonts and names carefully crafted into letterhead are aesthetically pleasing, but impossible to read.

10. Missing Information

People sometimes forget to list something as critical as a phone number or the name of the school they are attending.

11. Too Much Sharing

Do not include any information on your marital status, physical attributes, age, race, sex, sexual orientation, religion, creed, physical or mental disability, or any other characteristic that an employer cannot legally use to bar you from a job. Also, your social security number doesn't need to be on your résumé.

12. Poor Printing

If you're unfortunate enough to own an antiquated dot matrix printer, our condolences. Make sure you at least reink your ribbon before printing! Better yet, suck up the cost and laser print your résumés. At the very least, make one nice original and photocopy it. Don't photocopy old photocopies either.

13. Wrong Paper Choice

You want your résumé to be read—why make it difficult? Stick to white or cream colored paper. Avoid darker shades and textures. Many companies will photocopy or even scan your résumé. Dark or textured paper won't reproduce well, if at all. Onion-skin or typewriter paper may crinkle in a satisfactory manner, but it's too slippery to photocopy easily.

Sample Résumés

Now that we've discussed what to avoid when writing your résumé, let's try an exercise in résumé reading. The student Jonathan Miller has set his sights on an environmental consulting job. We'll be analyzing three different versions of his résumé. Here's the first one:

Jonathan L. Miller
PO Box 2425
Ivy University
Collegetown, MA 02114
tel: 617 555-3333
Email: jlm999@aaol.com
          killermiller@ivyu.edu

Objective: Environmental Consultant

Education:

Ivy University 1998, BA - Biology

Skills and experience:
Language skills: Fluent in French, familiar with Spanish and Latin.

Computer familiarity:

- Quite familiar with PCs and Macintosh including Microsoft Word, Excel, Claris Works, and PageMaker

Other skills:

- volunteer, with Habitat for Humanity & Clean Up the Harbor
- temporary office worker, handling phones and correspondence
- camp counselor, supervising children in outdoor camp
- intern, summer of unpaid project work in office setting

Work history:

94 - 98	Full-time student at Ivy	
97 (summer)	Intern	Boston, MA
92 - 93	Temporary worker	Washington, DC
90 - 93	Camp counselor	Washington, DC
90 - 97	Volunteer	Washington, DC

References: available upon request

Comments

The above résumé is a good example of what *not* to do when putting your résumé together. Here are some reasons why:

Address:
- Jonathan is a student. Unless you're going to be at your school address year-round, you really should include a permanent address. Companies may hold off on granting you a second interview if you are nowhere to be found.
- Why list two e-mail addresses when one will do?

Objective:
- While it's good to have an objective in mind when you create your résumé, it's not necessary to state the objective on the résumé itself. If you use one, make sure it's good. This objective is both too narrow and too broad at the same time. It doesn't tell the reader a whole lot. Jonathan might be better off with two résumés, one with no objective and one that gives a little more information about the kind of environmental consulting he's interested in.

Education:
- This doesn't tell us the whole story. Were Jonathan's grades really poor and is that why he didn't list them? Did he take any courses outside of his major? Any academic honors or awards? And where, exactly, is Ivy University?

Skills and Experience:
- This section is too broad. Why lump together skills and experience when they can be separated out?
- The skills/experiences are out of order. Jonathan's language skills are hardly applicable to a job as an environmental consultant, and he has listed them first. Generally speaking, skills should be listed in order of importance, and experience should be presented in chronological order, with the most recent experience first.
- He has put experience in with "skills." Jonathan's "Other skills" section, besides being poorly formatted, is a mess. What he has

done is list very briefly the jobs he mentions under work history. He's not listing skills, he's fleshing out his experiences.

- He has used organization names inconsistently. Why does Jonathan bother to name Habitat for Humanity and Clean up the Harbor, yet doesn't tell us the name of the summer camp or where he interned for a summer?

Work History:

- Volunteer work and school are listed under "work history." Why not add a section on "activities" instead? And Jonathan's four years as a biology student at Ivy really don't count as "work history."

Overall:

- Too little information! We appreciate the attempt to keep things brief, but this is bordering on sparse.
- The format doesn't make any sense. Why is education the only word highlighted?
- We don't get much of a sense of what Jonathan did during school. While filling a résumé with personal data is inappropriate, employers will want to know about any other skill-building experiences you've had, especially those that develop leaders and problem solvers.

Jonathan got some feedback, and resubmitted the résumé presented on the next two pages. It's closer, but still has some major flaws. Any ideas why?

Jonathan L. Miller
current address: permanent address
PO Box 2425 127 Maple Avenue
Ivy University Smalltown, MD 11211
Collegetown, MA 02114 404 555-2222
tel: 617 555-3333
Email jlm999@aaol.com or killermiller@ivyu.edu

Objective

A position in environmental consulting with a specialty in either transportation hazards or petroleum containment utilizing a course in which I gave a presentation on the impact of oil spills in the oceans as well as the hazards of petroleum leaks at truck stops along major interstates

Education

Ivy University in Collegetown, MA
BA, Biology with a minor in Environmental Studies, June 1998, 2.9 GPA

Experience

Coastal Consulting - Boston, MA
Jun - Sept 1997: Summer intern; performed all office functions including typing, filing, proofreading, and photocopying my supervisor's documents. Worked very closely with the project manager overseeing a study of the effects of oil spillage on Boston Harbor and the Charles River. This entailed keeping track of schedules for different employees, documenting all water samples taken and the results of the water once we studied the content of the sample, and taking new samples when some were misplaced. Also got to write first draft of summary remarks of our data. Headed a team of 8 other interns from other parts of the country. Checked in with the City of Boston on similar studies done in other metropolitan areas near major bodies of water.

Accountants on Call - Temporary Office worker - Washington, DC, Boston, MA
Jun 92 - Aug 93; Jun 94 - Aug 95; Held various accounting jobs throughout two cities on a full-time basis during the summers and part time during the school year. Worked in small CPA firm doing clerical work; helped in larger accounting firm with company audits. Mostly clerical duties but some exposure to balance sheets, accounts payable, and accounts receivable. Trained in Quicken and responsible for reconciling the books of one smaller firm.

Blue Ridge Summer Camp - Shenandoah Valley, VA
Summers 90 - 93; was a counselor for the 8 - 12 year old boys' cabin for three summers. Became a senior counselor, managing three junior counselors and two counselors in training. Managed the soccer program for all boys and was responsible for scheduling games and for founding the first ever end of the session tournament. Also responsible for providing my campers with recreational, social, and interpersonal guidance throughout the summer. Received the award for greatest contribution to camp life the summer of '93.

Habitat for Humanity, Clean up the Harbor - Washington, DC; Boston, MA
10/90 - present; volunteered for Habitat for Humanity in Washington DC mainly during the summers. Continued to be involved when I came to Boston for school. Clean up the Harbor has been a passion of mine for the last few years, especially in light of my research project last spring.

Other Experience

Pizzeriea Uno - Boston, MA
Part-time, Oct. '94 - Jun '97; busboy, host, and waiter at this busy, family-oriented Chicago style pizzeria with high volume. Promoted over time to positions of greater responsibility

Ivy U. Bartending Agency - Boston, MA
Sept '95 - present; part-time bartending and catering help for customers in need of anything from one keg to an entire open bar, for beer bashes and holiday parties. Developed customer service skills.

AYSO - Newton, MA
Sept 94 - present; volunteered as a coach for 10 - 13 year old boys for one season; referee on an as-needed basis for girls' and boys' leagues.

Skills

Language skills: Fluent in French, familiar with Spanish and Latin.
Computer familiarity: Quite familiar with PCs and Macintosh including Microsoft Word, Excel, Claris Works, and PageMaker. Limited experience with Quickbooks and some data entry programs.
Other: type 50 wpm, 9 key by touch, quick learner.

Activities

Lambda Chi Fraternity pledge master, vice president, and community impact officer. Varsity soccer.

References available upon request

30

Comments

Let's take a moment to discuss the problems with this second attempt.

Objective:
- In Jonathan's attempt to elaborate, he provided too much information. Also, it's a good idea to remove any personal pronouns ("in which I gave" doesn't belong on a résumé—in a cover letter, maybe).

Education:
- Does the GPA help or hurt? Some companies might have minimum GPA requirements (like a 3.0). If you omit your GPA, people may assume you're hiding something. It's your call, but if you think your grades will hurt your application, leave them off and be prepared to explain them in an interview.

Experience:
- The text is too uniform. Jonathan should try to highlight either the companies or the jobs he held—the way it is now, it's impossible to read quickly.
- The type is awfully dense and small. It's okay to use a small typeface if you alternate it with white space or a different font.
- Avoid huge blocks of text. This résumé would benefit a lot by breaking down the blurbs below the job titles into short statements highlighted by bullet points.
- The description under "Habitat for Humanity" doesn't belong. His comment about the harbor being a passion of his should be relegated to a cover letter.

Other Experience:
- The headings are confusing. Why use both "experience" and "other experience"?
- Are beer bashes necessarily appropriate for a résumé? We appreciate the logistics of having to tend bar at a beer bash, but the language is too informal.
- Typographical errors. Not only is Pizzeria spelled Pizzeriea, the description is missing a period at the end.

Skills:

- An unusual grouping of skills. It's confusing to lump "quick learner" in with office-related skills like "9 key" or typing speed. Jonathan's computer skills may be relevant for the type of job he seeks, but are his language skills? With too much information and not enough space, he will need to trim down a thing or two, and the language skills might be a likely candidate to cut.

Activities:

- Jonathan should devote more time to describing his activities. He should elaborate on some of the skills he may have picked up through his fraternity and athletic experiences; these are more relevant to prospective employers than most of the skills he mentions.

Overall:

- The margins and formatting make the résumé almost painful to read. The content of this résumé is actually pretty good, but it gets lost in the sea of words.
- Too much information! A résumé should only go over one page if the résumé writer has particularly impressive achievements to detail or, perhaps, a list of publications. Jonathan's résumé is certainly not in this category, and must be cut down to one page.

See what you think of Jonathan's third attempt, on the next page:

JONATHAN L. MILLER

P.O. Box 2425
Ivy University
Collegetown, MA 02114
tel: (617) 555-3333
email: killermiller@ivyu.edu

127 Maple Avenue
Smalltown, MD 11211
tel: (404) 555-2222

Education   IVY UNIVERSITY, Collegetown, MA,
B.A. Biology, expected 1998.
Minor in Environmental Studies.
Selected to read honor's thesis at environmental studies conference.

Experience   *Summer Intern*, Coastal Consulting, Boston, MA, Summer 1997
- Participated in a group study of the effects of oil spillage on Boston Harbor and the Charles River
- Headed a team of 6 interns from supervising schedules to reporting on our progress to management
- Acted as liasion to the City of Boston, writing the preliminary summary of the group's findings

Busboy, Host, Waiter; Pizzeria Uno, Boston, MA, 1995–1997
- Promoted over time to positions of greater responsibility

Bartender, Ivy U. Bartending Agency, Boston, MA, 1995–1997
- Developed customer service skills

Camp Counselor, Blue Ridge Camp, Shenandoah, VA, 1990–93
- Responsible for 4 counselors and a cabin of 12-year-old boys
- Managed soccer program; founded annual soccer tournament

Activities   *Vice President,* Lambda Chi Fraternity, 1995–1996
- Mentored a pledge class when pledge master abruptly quit
- Encouraged house to help in the annual clean-up of Boston Harbor; saw a 40% increase in number of volunteers

Division 1 Varsity Soccer, Ivy University, 1994–1995

Skills   Microsoft Word, Excel, PageMaker, Quickbooks, Internet

Personal   Youth soccer coach and referee
Volunteer for Habitat for Humanity and Clean up the Harbor

While Jonathan's third résumé isn't perfect, it provides us with a better picture of what Jonathan did during his undergraduate years, both inside and outside the classroom, and it is much better tailored to the type of environmental consulting job he is interested in. This version also has a much clearer and more attractive look than his previous attempts.

The Other Side of the Table

Recruiters at *SCORE!* have received all kinds of applications, including 10-stanza rhymed poetry, colorful gingerbread-man flyers saying, "Don't miss out on a great find!" and faxes announcing in a 1-2-3 blast-off countdown that an applicant's application is about to be transmitted. They've seen résumés on paper so bright it hurt to look at them. Such gimmicks are risky—they may appeal to some people, but the chances are good that they'll turn more people off.

So what should *your* résumé look like? There is no one right way for a résumé to look, but there are certain conventions that you should observe, especially as a relative neophyte on the job market. If you try to get too creative and/or cute, you may wind up sabotaging your chances of being called for an interview.

Look over the template on the next page to find out what the basic elements of a résumé are generally considered to be, and how many applicants go about filling in the blanks under the standard headings. Although the ways in which you list dates, job titles, and employers will vary according to the type of job you are seeking, the following is one good way of presenting a clear, uncluttered, and to-the-point résumé.

YOUR NAME
Your Own Street
Yourtown, ME 07556

Summary/ Objective (optional): Here's where you will describe in about 25 words who you are, what you specialize in, and what your main accomplishments are. If you are writing an objective, you will say what job you're after and try to sneak in a major quality or two.

Education: **Goodteach University**, Bennington, VT
B.A. English, 1993
Magna Cum Laude

Experience: **Most Recent Company**, Recentville, TX, Job Title, 1995 to present.
- Say what you accomplished.
- State what job entailed.
- Use phrases.
- Employ strong verbs.
- Use numbers.

Next Most Recent Company, Lasttown, MI, Job Title, 1993–1995.
- Note how you helped your boss save money.
- Use tight, to-the-point phrases.
- See pattern above.

Your First Job, Firsttown, WY, Job Title, Summer 1993
- Say what you did to help.
- More of what you did.

Personal/ References/ Skills (choose one): Here's where you note an outside interest that tells the reader about some positive quality that may be relevant to his/her needs. Or you will say, "Available upon request," if you are doing a reference line. For skills, you might list some relevant skills not evident elsewhere on the résumé, such as the ability to speak a foreign language.

Now that we've looked at some ways of formatting a résumé, let's discuss what goes into it. As a student, you will probably have to think about experience in a somewhat different way than the majority of job applicants do.

What "Experience" Means For You

What are you thinking at this moment? Perhaps something along the lines of "I don't have any experience! What are they talking about? I've been a student, and nobody wants to hire a student who doesn't have any experience!"

Writing a résumé can be an intimidating prospect for students because, by definition, they don't have much work experience to draw upon. However, keep in mind that even if you've never worked, you still have "experience." You've had a full-time job for quite some time—school. You've been working at applying yourself in your studies. And during your four or more years in college, you've probably gained experience in more areas than you realize.

We've broken your background down into three areas—academics, work experience, and activities. In each of these areas, you've had to apply yourself, develop skills, and be resourceful. The following will help you determine which examples from these areas to highlight on your résumé:

Academics

Whatever your major, you were involved in study groups, sections, and possibly even a senior thesis or oral project. Studying a particular subject exposes you to various work environments. Did you participate in group research projects or, perhaps, a multidisciplinary independent study? If so, would it benefit you to mention that on your résumé? Did you double major? Do you have a minor or a concentration? Did you take any unusual courses outside your major that might apply to your intended field?

Unless you majored in engineering or computer science (in which case potential employers might need to see all courses taken), there's no reason to include a long list of courses taken. If you feel the need to provide your coursework, why not include a transcript and save space for more relevant information?

Did you receive any academic awards or scholarships? What kind of grades did you get? Is your GPA stronger in your major? Did you improve significantly in your final two years? Did you work all four years and have to sacrifice your grade point average to cover tuition or living expenses?

Work Experience

The first thing you need to do is make a list of all of the jobs you've had. Don't worry if it was only a one-night catering job or two afternoons of painting a house. You won't include all of these on your résumé, but it might be helpful for you to remember that you really liked the chance to make your own hours, work outdoors, and/or work on weekends so you could go to school during the week.

If you worked steadily throughout school in jobs that are not career-related, you may still want to include them very briefly to explain to a potential employer that you were industrious and hard-working and aren't afraid of entry-level work (if, of course, that's true).

Once you've decided which jobs to list on the résumé, you'll need to decide how to list them. This will depend on the kind of job for which you're applying, as we saw when we analyzed Jonathan Miller's résumé. Because Jonathan was interested in an environment-oriented job, he listed his Coastal Consulting internship first, and downplayed his waiting experience.

Activities

Are there any activities, employment, volunteering, sports involvement, or other extracurriculars in which you've been involved? Some examples: involvement in campus organizations such as fraternities or sororities,

37

Hidden Experience

Many college seniors say that they have no experience in a particular area (such as sales, public speaking, leadership, delegation, problem solving, or project management) when it becomes clear after a few minutes of conversation that some of the activities in which they've engaged helped develop exactly these kind of skills.

student government, dormitory councils, newspapers, debating societies, a cappella groups, orientation programs, community volunteering, undergraduate business societies, tour guiding, and residential education. This is one area that students often ignore in looking for a job.

Again, you'll need to consider the nature of the job you're trying to get before determining exactly which activities will go on your résumé. Choose your examples wisely.

COVER LETTERS

Cover letters seem to instill in the job seeker a sense of dread almost as strong as that brought on by résumé writing. But writing a cover letter is the best part of an application. The only time you should really feel nervous about it is if you haven't done enough research to know such basics as the name of the person to whom you're writing, the job for which you're applying, and why you're a good fit for that job. If you know those three things, you'll be fine. If you don't, then there's a strong possibility that either this isn't the job for you, or you need to go back and do some homework to understand why it is.

Why, you may be asking yourself, is the cover letter the best part of an application? A résumé has to be one page of information that's specific enough to help you land a job but general enough for you to give to more than one company. You probably won't have ten versions of your résumé for ten different firms; instead, you write one that's just generic or specific enough to make do for all ten. Cover letters, on the other hand, allow you to:

- Tailor your application to a specific audience
- Demonstrate sincere interest in and knowledge of a company

- Infuse your application with personality and enthusiasm
- Show off your writing skills and persuasiveness
- Drop names
- Provide details not on your résumé
- Explain *why* you want to work for the company

You never know what will happen with a carefully crafted résumé. Odds are good that it won't even be read that carefully. But cover letters get you in the door. Try submitting a résumé without a cover letter, and you'll most likely discover that it won't get very far.

Most of the guides to writing résumés also cover how to write an effective cover letter. The most successful cover letters are short and to the point; they relate how the applicant heard about the company and why he or she wants to work for the company, as well as provide a quick rundown of why the company would want him or her as an employee. It's okay to mention one or two points covered on your résumé, but try to vary the language a little. *Cover letters should never merely restate your résumé.*

The Essential Cover Letter

The only time you can get away with submitting a résumé *without* a cover letter is if you've gotten an interview by signing up for on-campus interviews through bidding. It's not a bad idea to write the letter anyway. Going through the process of explaining why you want to work for a company is an excellent exercise. Besides, you'll have something to give to the employer when you arrive, and they'll have a reason to remember you.

A cover letter should be written in the same font and printed on the same paper as your résumé. If that's not possible, stick with white paper and a common font (Times, Palatino, or Geneva). These letters should always be typed. Three-page, handwritten cover letters on yellow lined notebook paper, or three sticky notes attached to a carelessly folded résumé, are definitely not appropriate. And remember that a fax cover sheet does not count as a cover letter.

Sample Cover Letters

It's now time to analyze the cover letter that Jonathan Miller has drafted to go with his résumé. See if you can identify any problems with the following effort:

January 15, 1998

Jonathan L. Miller
PO Box 2425
Ivy University
Collegetown, MA 02114
617 555-3333

To whom it may concern:

I am about to graduate from Ivy University and am interested in the opening listed with your firm. I have good language skills, computer skills, I learn quickly, and I am very hard-working. Although I have very little work experience outside of summer and internship experience, I feel that your company could be a great fit for me.

I can be reached at the above telephone number and am very interested in hearing from you at your earliest convenience.

Thank you.

Sincerely,

Jonathan Miller

Comments

This generic, brief letter tells us absolutely nothing about why Jonathan would be a good candidate. It does, however, give some major hints as to why he might not be worth an interview. Writing a cover letter is like a lot of things in life. You just might get out of it what you put into it. How much effort did Jonathan put into this letter? And what kind of results do you think he might expect?

Format:
- Jonathan's letter has inconsistent formatting. He has lined every-thing (the date, the address, and the body of the letter) up with the left margin except the signature. Make sure you review proper business-letter formatting. In general, consistency is most impor-tant. If you don't like the look of everything lined up on the left, it's okay to right align the date. But if you do, you'll also need to right align the "Sincerely," and your signature.
- Jonathan's spacing is off as well. If he's going to leave out the com-pany's address on the top of the letter (not a good idea), he should start the greeting a few lines up. He should also double-check the number of lines between the paragraphs—there's an extra space between the last two paragraphs.

Greeting:
- If at all possible, you should send your letter and résumé to a spe-cific person. If you cannot find the title of someone in human resources, personnel, or recruiting (by going to the career center, looking at the Web site or calling the company), at least put in "Hiring Manager" or "On-Campus Recruiter."

The Generic Kiss of Death:
- Do you know what position Jonathan is interested in pursuing? It's "the opening," but what if this particular company is adver-tising more than one job listing? And at which company? There's no company address at the start, and in the body of the letter he refers to "your firm" and "your company." This looks like a form letter that Jonathan is cranking out and sending to a stack of ads.

What's In It For Me?

- Not only does he make no effort to customize this letter to a particular company, he's missing a critical opportunity to sell himself. Jonathan gives a brief rundown of some uniform skills and then states, "your company is a great fit for me," although he admits that he has little experience. Hiring managers, if they've gotten this far, will be wondering: What's in it for the company to give this guy an interview? Based on this letter, not much.

The Signature:

- This is a small detail, but Jonathan will need tiny writing to fit his signature in the space that's been allotted. Not to mention the fact that he hasn't signed the letter, a common mistake.

On this page and the next you'll find a second attempt. Do you think it does a better job?

January 15, 1998

Jonathan L. Miller
PO Box 2425
Ivy University
Collegetown, MA 02114
617 555-3333

Awesome Environment Consulting Co.
2399 Commonwealth Avenue, Suite C
Boston, MA 02110

Dear Hiring Manager,

I am about to graduate from Ivy University with a BA in Biology and a minor in Environmental Studies. I will be finished in June, 1998. I came across your ad dated January 8, 1998 in the career center at school and I'm writing now to express my sincere interest in this opportunity.

In addition to coursework which is relevant to the environmental consulting position, I also have some work experience which has helped me prepare for the opportunity to work at Awesome Environment. Specifically, I have been an active volunteer with Habitat for Humanity and Clean up the Harbor. You will notice from my resume that I have worked in a busy restaurant setting, I've been a bartender, and also a camp counselor. I also held an office in my fraternity for two years. I competed in varsity soccer for one year as well. I've continued to be active in the community through my role as a soccer coach and referee. I find the referee job especially rewarding because I get to educate parents on the importance of encouraging and supporting their children's efforts. Working in an environmental consulting company would give me an opportunity to educate people on another important issue.

I have a history of working hard to get the job done, whatever the job may entail. If you're looking for a dedicated, hard-working employee who will do whatever it takes, please look no further. I'm looking for a company in which to develop professionally and to contribute my skills, my enthusiasm, and my work ethic. I feel that Awesome Environment Consulting could be such a place.

I notice that you'll be coming to campus for interviews at the end of winter quarter. I would very much like to meet with you at that time or on another date if that's more convenient for you. You can reach me at the number above.

Thank you for taking the time to review my résumé.

Sincerely,

Jonathan L. Miller

Comments

This cover letter is better, but it could use some editing.

Reiterating the Résumé:
- A cover letter allows you to explain or elaborate on details of your application that aren't necessarily on your résumé. While it's okay to touch on a few highlights of the résumé that are relevant to the application, you do *not* want to present your résumé in prose form. Jonathan gave us some interesting information, but for the most part he has repackaged his résumé.

Brief is Better:
- While the first letter Jonathan wrote was too brief, this letter is much too wordy. As with résumés, it's not advisable to go over a page. Not only is the letter too long, it doesn't convey a sense of why Jonathan is suited for this job or why he should stand out from a field of applicants.

Layout:
- The spacing is still a bit off on the address section of the letter, and the margins are rather small.

With only a little reworking, however, this could be an effective letter. See if you approve of the edits Jonathan made on this second draft to produce his final cover letter, found on the next page.

January 15, 1998

Jonathan L. Miller
P.O. Box 2425
Ivy University
Collegetown, MA 02114
(617) 555-3333

Awesome Environment Consulting Co.
2399 Commonwealth Avenue, Suite C
Boston, MA 02110

Dear Hiring Manager,

Your ad for an Environmental Consultant position immediately caught my eye. I've had two passions for much of my life: soccer and the environment. It's been my dream to pursue a future built around one of them. After a career-ending knee injury dashed my hopes of playing soccer professionally, I threw myself into my studies and resolved to develop skills that could be applied to a job in environmental consulting. The day I presented my honor's thesis on the hazards of transporting petroleum products to the department's annual conference, I was proud to be the only student presenter. And I knew I'd found my calling.

You seek someone who is flexible, hard-working, interested in growth with the company, and who has an interest in the environment. My restaurant experience taught me about the importance of self-motivation. I've sought and been awarded positions of leadership, partly because I love encouraging my peers, whether it's to score a goal in a close soccer match or to sign up a reluctant volunteer for our fraternity's Saturday clean-up efforts. And whether it's an internship or volunteer opportunity, I've worked for the environment every chance I've had. In short, I'm your man.

I would very much like to meet with you when you visit our campus, or before then if that's more convenient for you. I will be available to begin work on July 1st. You can reach me at (617) 333-3333. I look forward to hearing from you!

Sincerely,

Jonathan Miller

Comments

- This letter is still a bit long, but it is full of information that either wasn't on the résumé or isn't immediately clear. If you're deciding on how much information to put in your cover letter, keep in mind that it depends on how much selling you think you need to do to land the interview. If you've already had a twenty-minute conversation with a recruiter on the phone, you can probably keep it short and sweet. If, however, you're going for one of a few coveted interview slots on campus, it won't hurt to state your case.
- As was mentioned earlier, Jonathan really should try to get the name of the campus recruiter. If he knows a company representative is coming to campus, he should check with the career center to see who will conduct interviews.

COMPLETING YOUR APPLICATION

A few more elements need to be added to your résumé before you send it off to the company you're interested in working for:

References

It's common for people to put a line at the bottom of the résumé: "References available upon request." If you're worried about space, you might delete this line and prepare a references sheet that's done in the same font and on the same paper as your résumé. When listing references, it's good to give the name and phone number of the reference (addresses are optional), and to indicate whether it's a personal or a professional reference. You won't need to hand these out at each interview, but if you tell someone you're happy to provide references and then, when asked to do so, are forced to comb through an old address book that is missing important things like phone numbers, the good impression that you're trying to make may be damaged.

Choosing your references is more than a one-step process. You'll need to identify whom to use, contact them to make sure they're willing to talk to people, and then—and this is something that is often neglected—prep your references on what they should say. If you're looking for a particular kind of job, or if you'd like them to highlight a particular skill or experience, tell them so. Let them know who might be contacting them. Once you hand out your references to someone, it's always good to make a follow-up phone call to that reference, especially if it has been a while since you asked them to speak for you.

Transcripts

The most commonly requested "other piece of information" is a copy of your transcript. Transcripts usually cost $2–$6 to order. Some schools require written requests, and some take quite a while to process. Your best bet will be to order and have on hand official copies (printed on official paper, often with a raised seal, special inks, or noncopyable paper to ensure authenticity) and unofficial copies as well (as simple as a photocopy of an official copy or, in some cases, an unofficial list of courses taken and grades received that you can print from the Internet). Some companies will be fine with an unofficial copy to begin the process, but will require an official copy down the line; others require an official copy from the start.

Job Applications

As we mentioned in the section on career fairs and info sessions, some companies will have formal applications for you to fill out. Job applications often ask for the same information you've already put on your résumé. They might also ask about geographic preferences, drug tests, references, salary history, and so on. Most companies will let you know during the interview process if you need to fill out an application.

Apply Online

Some companies allow you to fill out an application online. Check out the Enterprise Rent a Car site (at http://www.erac.com/recruit/ResumeForm.asp) or *SCORE!*'s Web site (http://www.score.kaplan.com) for examples of online applications.

Letters of Recommendation

If you have them and they're strong, it won't hurt to provide them. If they're not all that glowing, you might hold off on barraging a recruiter with tons of paper. These are sometimes nice things to add in a thank you letter to a recruiter—it gives you a reason to follow up.

Work Samples

If you're applying for something creative, ask if the interviewer would like to see samples of your work. Sometimes it's acceptable to submit writing samples, drawings, sketches, or even audio tapes (if you're a musician). And in certain fields, such as the creative side of advertising, it's expected. If you show up without a portfolio, you'll need to have a good reason why.

More Help, If You Need It

Kaplan and Simon & Schuster's book *Résumé Builder & Career Counselor* is a useful resource to help you create your résumé. Author Anna Murray does an especially good job of walking you through your past experiences, calling attention to the best way to describe what you've done and to format it clearly.

It's never easy to boil yourself down to a résumé and a letter. Remember that all of the other applicants have to do the same thing. Your goal is to get your foot in the door, whether it's through amazing references, some unusual overseas travel, or a refreshing, effective cover letter. Your application is the key that unlocks the door to the interview room. How you find out which companies have doors to unlock is another story. That'll be the subject of the next chapter.

section **2**

THE INTERVIEW

chapter 5
LANDING AN INTERVIEW

By now, you have probably registered with your career center, identified industries and/or companies that interest you, and written a résumé targeted at a particular position or field. Now it's time to speak with employers. There are two main ways to arrange for an interview with a company—go through sign-ups for on-campus interviews at the career center, or contact companies directly.

ON-CAMPUS INTERVIEWING

Attend orientations for students participating in on-campus interviews and read any materials given to you before getting started. That way, you'll know the procedures for scheduling an interview with a company recruiter.

Go to your career center (online or in person), and study the list of on-campus recruiters. Check out the company binders. Even if you don't think you'll find anything you like, look anyway. Go back through the literature you picked up at the career fair and look for any job descriptions that appeal to you. Begin to identify those that interest you and become familiar with the job descriptions for which you qualify. Pay attention to the information sessions coming up at your school. Info sessions are one of the best ways of learning more about opportunities within a company.

Most career centers hold on-campus interviews every term. If you're on a quarter system, you might have three interview seasons—fall, winter, and spring. Schools on a semester calendar will set up fall and spring schedules. There are exceptions: Small schools sometimes hold interviews only once a year, and some schools will restrict part or all of one season to one field (such as accounting). Anyone who commits to participating in on-campus interviews will need to be aware of certain deadlines which, as with your course load, will depend a lot on whether you're on a quarter or semester schedule. The number of seasons a career center arranges will depend on how interested employers are in your school.

Every career center has its own scheduling system. You may find yourself signing up over the phone using voicemail, through a computer via the Internet, or in person at the career center. Regardless of how you actually get your name on the list, there are several distinct kinds of interview schedules that schools use: employer preselect schedules, bidding, open scheduling, or some combination of the three.

Employer Preselect Schedules

These schedules give applicants the chance to turn in résumés well in advance of the company's on-campus interview date. The career center sends all collected résumés to the company. Recruiters or company representatives sort through them and preselect a group of students to interview. The career center contacts the appropriate students and schedules the appointments.

The criteria used to weed out résumés will depend on the type of job being filled, but GPA, work experience, leadership experience, extracurricular or volunteer involvement, and technical skills are often deciding factors. Not to mention typos in résumés or cover letters.

The benefit of preselecting a company (sometimes referred to as résumé dropping—meaning that you drop your résumé in the company's file before the drop deadline) is that you don't lose anything by doing so, other than the time spent in preparing your résumé and cover letter.

52

It's Not the End of the World

Don't give up on a company you're really interested in just because you weren't preselected. While it is possible that you don't have the qualifications and background the company is looking for, there's also a chance that you were number eight on its list and it could only select six candidates. Try to interview through bidding for any remaining interview slots, or see if you can be put on a waiting list.

Since some schools restrict the number of candidates a recruiter may preselect to half of their overall appointments, preselect interviews can sometimes be tough to get (if an employer has 12 interviews scheduled but can choose only six students out of the 80 résumés that came in, your odds aren't great).

Bidding

Bidding schedules are a bit like a lottery. You're given a certain number of points or priority bids that you can then bid on interview slots as soon as sign-ups begin for a particular company's interview schedule. If there's one company with which you are determined to interview, you might want to place all of your points on getting that interview. If you'd be happy talking to any of the ten accounting firms coming on campus, a better strategy might be to spread your points out among a few of them. Once again, check with your career center to see what they advise. In some cases, companies will return to campus throughout the course of the year. That's something to keep in mind when deciding how to use your points.

The Other Side of the Table

Because students don't risk anything by dropping a résumé, recruiters are sometimes overwhelmed by applicants for preselect dates. When this happens, recruiters become wary of applicants who look like they may be dropping résumés indiscriminately. Include a cover letter with your résumé, a letter that demonstrates your familiarity with what the company is looking for and, if this is not apparent from your résumé, why you'd be a good fit for the job. Anything you can do to make yourself stand out from the piles of résumés a recruiter must wade through is worth your time.

Open Schedules

Open schedules are just that—open to anyone who wishes to sign up. Usually filled on a first-come-first-served basis, they allow people to sign up for interview slots without being preselected by the company or bidding any points.

Before You Commit Yourself to a Strategy . . .

Your goal should be to utilize the on-campus interviewing opportunities available to you to the utmost while remaining considerate of the needs of other students. Before you decide on your résumé-dropping or bidding strategy, there are a few factors you might want to take into account.

Are Well-Known Companies a Good Choice or Not?

Certain companies always fill up their schedules and create huge waiting lists, while other smaller, less well-known companies might have openings the day of the interview. Big name firms will inspire more competition among the students. You might want to think about your chances of landing the interview with the established firm over trying an up-and-coming company.

Are "Practice" Interviews a Good Idea?

It may be tempting to line up "practice" interviews—meetings with the companies you wouldn't really want to work for, but know you could talk to or might learn from. But be considerate of the other students who might be genuinely interested, not to mention of the recruiters' time. Some career centers will allow you to practice your interviewing skills with counselors.

Your Job Search Versus Your Workload

If you know that winter quarter will be crammed full of classes, structuring a job search that includes researching and résumé writing in the fall and interviewing in the spring might be a wise choice. Your time is valuable, and the last thing you want to do is stretch yourself to the point where you neither find a job nor do well in classes.

Be Realistic When You Drop Your Résumé

If you want to work for a big bank, make sure you have a sense of any requirements ahead of time (such as GPA, major, etcetera). You don't want to waste your points getting interviews that won't go anywhere. Your career center may be able to fill you in on how the previous class did, including which majors were considered for a position.

Interview On Campus, If At All Possible

If you go through the career center's on-campus program, you'll save yourself the headache of contacting companies, arranging interviews, and all of the phone calling and message leaving that go with it.

Don't Forget Waiting Lists

If an open interview schedule fills up before you can get your name on it, don't give up. You can always call or stop by the career center to put your name on a waiting list. Waiting lists are useful for two reasons. If there is a cancellation prior to the day of the interview, you just might get lucky. Alternatively, if the recruiter takes a look at the wait-listed candidates and likes your résumé, you might get a call about setting something up at another time.

Landing the interviews of your choice doesn't always work out according to plan. You might get wait-listed, but never make it onto the schedule. You might not fit the criteria for the job. There may be too many others who bid more points. There are lots of explanations as to why you may not get the interview of your choice. Before you give up in disgust, you should remember that you're a student with access to information that will help you. All of those things we mentioned earlier—a great job market, your research skills, the resources available, and the fact that some companies are actively seeking strong college seniors—still apply. You'll just have to work a little harder.

OTHER SOURCES FOR INTERVIEWS

In chapters 1 and 2, we gave you an overview of on-campus recruitment and the career center. You should have a clear picture of the services your school offers. Some of the events we mentioned are possible sources for landing an interview, particularly if you've moved out of the "what's out there, anyway?" to the "I know what I want to do—who's looking for someone like that?" phase of your search. Let's take a closer look at some familiar things:

Career Fairs

Certain companies are popular, well-known recruiters on campus and will have a professional, systematic approach to the interested applicant. At the career fair, these companies' tables will be three deep in potential recruits and will most likely have a sign up sheet for an information session. Other organizations wish to hire one or two people for the year and may not have a formal presentation or process in place at all. In the first case you may have to take a number to speak briefly with the company representative or, in the latter case, you might find yourself in an animated, 15-minute discussion.

Pay close attention to any job listings or company literature you picked up at the career fair. A company may advertise an opening that's not being filled through on-campus interviews. You should walk away from the table with either a business card or contact info for the company's college recruiter. If you're interested in interviewing with the company but aren't able to get in through on-campus interviews, why not write a letter expressing your interest in and suitability for a position at the company, and send it in with a résumé?

Also, keep in mind that most students stop by career fairs during lunch. If you're able to drop in earlier or later, you'll get more attention.

It's a great idea to bring a résumé with you. But don't skip out on the fair just because you haven't updated it recently or don't have copies. You can always pick up a business card or company contact information and send a résumé with a brief letter as a follow-up to the fair. Some compa-

The Other Side of the Table

Think about the career fair from the recruiters' point of view. They're probably tired. They've traveled a fair distance and will be talking to many people over the course of the day. This is *not* the time to stand squarely in front of the table, fire off 25 in-depth questions, and monopolize their time. The purpose of the fair is to learn more about opportunities, but use your head. These people will answer your questions, but they're also taking notes. What kind of first impression would you like to make?

nies will have info sheets or sign up sheets, and will happily send you notice of their info sessions.

Information Sessions

These meetings are closely linked with on-campus interview dates and provide information to prospective interviewees. Still, they're worth your time, even if you're not interviewing with the company on campus. You'll gain valuable information about the company's prospects, a sense of the company culture, and contact information which you can use to get in touch with the company on your own. And sometimes a well-written plea to a recruiter to consider squeezing in one more interview after on-campus dates, paired with the right résumé, might get you in the door.

Some companies will ask you to fill out an application before the info session to see if your profile meets that of the ideal candidate they're looking for. These can often be picked up at the career fair or in your college's career center. Chances are good that if you didn't see one in either of these two places, you won't need to fill out an application in advance.

If you were able to get company literature at the career fair or in the career center, make sure you read it. Visit the company's Web site if possible. But whatever you do, make sure that you have a preliminary grasp of what the company does and why you might be interested in working there. You may not get the chance to show off your

The Other Side of the Table

While company representatives tend to be busy presenting information and fielding questions, an info session is often an informal means of selecting strong candidates or eliminating weak ones. Most recruiters have very little time to do more than make a few quick observations. The more help you give them in assessing you, the better. This is why you need to bring a résumé, an informed sense of what the company does, and a few intelligent questions to make you stand out. You may have the chance to speak with a company representative after the presentation. And that conversation could determine whether or not you interview with the company.

knowledge, but you'll be ahead of the game if you take the time to do a little research.

Be on time. The recruiters made an effort to show up—so should you. If an info session is scheduled to begin at 7:00 P.M., don't stroll in at 7:20. Most people are understanding if you have a class conflict, but you need to remember that you are giving recruiters very few chances to get to know you. Recruiters are sometimes so busy that they're looking for excuses to eliminate people just to lessen the volume of paperwork they have to sort through. Don't blow your chances by disregarding the rules of common courtesy.

Sending Your Résumé Directly to the Recruiter

Let's assume you either chose not to participate in the on-campus interview program or were unable to get an interview with the company of your choice. It's not time to throw in the towel yet. You know the organization is willing to hire grads from your school and that they're active recruiters. It's a long shot, but if you're serious about wanting to work for a particular company, go ahead and send a résumé and letter directly to the recruiter on the off chance that the company hasn't hired its quota of graduates. If you do decide to pursue this tactic, you should have a good explanation as to why you're interested in the company and why you didn't interview on campus.

Web Sites

More and more companies are starting to list employment opportunities on their Web sites. If you're interested in a company that's not coming on campus, you should look over the site to see if there are any opportunities listed.

Online Job Listings

These services vary, ranging from those that upload your résumé and try to match you with a prospective employer to databases of job listings that are searchable by industry, location, or key words that appear in the job descriptions. Listings may be updated weekly, daily, or throughout the day. The Web has become riddled with job listing services, many of which cater specifically to the needs of recent grads. Take a look at the appendix at the back of this book to learn more about these sites.

Classified Ads

Your college paper's classified ads section might be a good source for part-time work during the school year. If you want full-time work, go to a larger newspaper. Looking at the ads on a regular basis will show you who is hiring and for what positions. These ads are also helpful if you're planning on relocating after school. You can easily find a copy of your destination city's newspaper.

Try not to rely solely on want ads—they have their drawbacks. Because the ads reach a large and probably more experienced audience, the competition may be stiff. Ads may also continue to run after the position has been filled. Many jobs listed in the classifieds require more experience or less education than you have. If you use them as a tool and not as the only resource for your job search, they may prove helpful.

"College Graduates"

Some papers, such as the *New York Times,* have started a section for "College Graduates" in addition to the more traditional job breakdowns. This is a good place for recent grads to look for jobs which may not require quite as much work experience as other listings.

59

Job Hotlines

Job hotlines are recordings or voicemail messages that list job opportunities at a specific organization. Because they're easy to update and an efficient way of giving out the same information over and over, they're convenient for companies. How do you find out the numbers? When you scan the want ads, look for shorter ads reading: "Call our job hotline to hear updated openings." Call corporate headquarters and see if a job hotline is one of your menu options, or keep an eye out for job hotlines listed in any media coverage of the company. Some college career centers use job hotlines as a way to check the most recent listings. These numbers will list new opportunities for a variety of listings, while a company job hotline will list opportunities within one company.

Employment Agencies

You can register with an agency in the business of matching employers with prospective employees. These agencies may charge you a fee, although often the companies using the service pay a percentage of a hired employee's salary as a finder's fee. Agencies may be looking to fill immediate openings rather than jobs that will become available in the summer.

You should be able to locate a few other sources of job listings by visiting your career center's library. Look for information on employment opportunities overseas, government jobs, private school teaching, and so forth.

UNLISTED OPPORTUNITIES

Many people are hired every year without ever responding to a formal job listing. How do they find out about unlisted opportunities? Word of mouth is a powerful means of communication. Employers often announce job openings internally before going to want ads, online job listings, or employment agencies. As a result, current employees or their friends, family, or colleagues will find out about openings first. Companies like to hire candidates referred by an employee. Some companies even pay referral bonuses to encourage people to tell their network of friends about the job. It's a great arrangement—the candidate already knows about the company and its culture, and the company has a recommendation from one of its employees. If you're wondering how you're ever going to discover hidden opportunities, the answer is simple . . . you have to network.

Networking

You're firmly rooted in one of the best networks around. Think about it—checked out a new movie recently? Read any good books? Taken any amazing classes this term? If you answered yes to any of these questions, answer this: How did you hear about the movie, book, or not-to-miss class? Information gets around via word of mouth both on campus and in the outside world.

Discovering opportunities requires some effort on your part. Don't just sit back and wait for someone to happen to mention that the most amazing job, which is tailor-made for you, has just become available. If you do, you'll be waiting for a long, long time. Tell everyone you know what you're looking for, and your chances of finding the right people to talk to increase enormously. Successful networkers know how to spread news quickly and to the right people.

You have many more potential advocates than you might think. Your professor of economics, for example, might have heard of an opening for a numbers-oriented person. But how is he supposed to know you're looking for a job if you don't tell him? Here's a list of other people whose opinions you should seek out:

What is "Networking?"

(a) Another name for ABC, NBC, CBS, and FOX

(b) A concept that's foreign to you because you don't like schmoozing with people or dropping names

(c) The way a lot of people find out about job openings

(Answer = (c))

- Immediate family
- Extended family
- Your family members' colleagues
- Neighbors
- Your hairdresser
- Your car mechanic
- Your doctor
- Your RA
- Your faculty advisor
- Your student advisor
- Your friends
- Alumni

Alumni

The last point is worth exploring further. You should know a few alums from classes, the dorms, Greek or club affiliations, jobs you held on campus, or other activities. Do you have any idea what these people are doing now? This is a great pool to explore if you're interested in learning about the reality of the job in a particular field. In addition to alumni in your peer group, you should have access to alums who have volunteered to act as resources to undergraduates.

Going to the alumni office or to the career center would be a good place to start. Here are some resources you might want to check out:

- Databases of alumni who are professional contacts (often sortable by field, location, or major)
- Alumni "mentors" who provide guidance and who will discuss their experiences
- Alumni whose companies are offering internships
- Shadowing or externship programs where you can follow an alum for a period of time or work in the company for a brief period
- Alumni networks for career advising

While alumni may willingly act as resources, do not abuse the privilege. If you expect to ride the wave of nostalgia about your alma mater all the way in to a job offer, think again. The chances of someone handing you a plum job on a silver platter are slim. Alumni contacts should not be regarded as sources for jobs. You should set your sights on an alumni contact resulting in an informational interview or a chance to receive some advice. And who knows? If you make a good impression, you may just be the person they think of the next time their company or one of their colleague's companies is hiring.

If you're going to school in one part of the country, but plan on moving home or relocating after school, alumni contacts may be especially valuable for you. Colleges often have regional chapters of their alumni associations, many of which have "young alumni" branches. On occasion, someone within the organization will even coordinate a networking committee. It would be a good idea to check with the alumni office to see if such a group exists and, if so, who the contact person might be. That way, you'll have a contact in your destination city who might be able to advise you on hiring trends within that region.

Regardless of how you locate an alum who works in the field of your choice, finding one is helpful. We mentioned that companies like to go on referrals from employees. Without that personal endorsement, an unknown applicant is exactly that—unknown. But if you happen to have attended the alma mater of the company's highly successful head of marketing, who has acted as a liaison for the alumni office and a lookout for bright new talent, so much the better.

Always take the time to thank the person whose time you've taken, and do it immediately. Write a quick note saying thank you. Send an e-mail or leave a message if for some reason you can't put pen to paper. Something as seemingly inconsequential as that two-minute letter could open or close doors for you.

Informational Interviews

Successful networkers uncover people willing to talk about their field of interest or their career choice. That conversation is what people call an "informational interview." The purpose of the informational interview is to meet with someone to gather information about them—their field, their company, their interests, their job, and their insights on what they do.

Informational interviews are also about contacts. Rarely will that first initial contact result in a job. Once you've spent 15 to 30 minutes speaking with someone, thank him for his time and ask him if he can recommend anyone else in his field who might be willing to talk to you. You may have to go through three or four levels of referrals before you finally find the person who keeps you in mind until she hears of a suitable opening, and offers you a job interview.

Other Sources

In addition to your personal networking contacts, you have some other methods of sleuthing available to you. You could haul out the Yellow Pages and cold-call 20 advertising agencies to get their human resources contact names (although we wouldn't necessarily recommend that). You might also clip an article on an up-and-coming Internet public relations firm and then, after hearing their VP of marketing interviewed on the radio, send your cover letter and résumé, and make a follow-up phone call.

When a company is written up in the press, its growth potential is often described. Brand new, emerging companies are often featured. In addition, the names of people working within a particular department are sometimes given. If you're really interested and have done your research, send a letter and résumé. Even if the company is not hiring right now, it might keep you in mind for the future. This approach probably works better with small or high growth companies than with big organizations that have an established maze of human resources departments.

HOW TO ASK FOR AN INTERVIEW

Once you have names, titles, phone numbers, and company names, the next step is to actually contact the appropriate people. These calls are tough—it's natural to choke up a little when asking someone for something—but they get better with practice and if you have a strategy. When calling someone to inquire about a résumé you've sent in, to schedule an informational interview, or to ask for a job interview, you need to follow some simple steps.

Before You Call

Set a goal for the conversation. Make sure that your reason for calling is clear in your mind before you get started. That way, you'll avoid stammering.

Have a pen that works and paper to write on. You may need to take notes, and it's not a good idea to make someone wait while you dig through the pile of pens that don't work.

Spit out your chewing gum. Try not to rustle paper. Sound carries remarkably well over the phone.

During the Call

If you get voicemail or a receptionist, leave a message. Don't forget such vital information as your name, telephone number, reason for calling, and how you heard about them. Be as brief and as confident as you can. Don't be afraid to follow up on messages you've left. Beware of babble! People appreciate brief, to-the-point messages. If you have a tendency to go on and on, especially when you're nervous, write down the main points of what you want to say. You'll get better with practice, but don't be afraid to use crutches.

Greet the person in a confident voice, but don't shout or race through the conversation. People sometimes talk loudly and more rapidly when they're nervous. Be sure to explain how you got the number: Are you responding to a job listing? Did a friend or a mutual acquaintance give you the person's name and number? If so, say so.

A Sample Message

"Hi, this is Jonathan Miller. I got your name from Don Jacobs who suggested I call you because I'm about to graduate with a major in environmental studies. Don thought you might be looking for someone with my background.

"I have worked for a consulting firm, and I'd love to talk to you about this. I also wanted to confirm that you got the résumé I sent you late last week. My telephone number is 555-3333. I'll try calling you back in one week if I haven't heard from you.

"I look forward to speaking with you. Thank you for your time."

65

We've already mentioned that you should keep the conversation brief and to the point. However, if you find that the person with whom you're speaking is in a chatty mood or wishes to learn more about you, take advantage of that and tell him what he wants to know. Just be sensitive about time.

If someone is too busy to talk to you, try to schedule a time that's more convenient for him. If necessary, call back again. How pushy should you be? That's up to you and the thickness of your skin. Sometimes people don't return calls because they're busy, not because they don't want to talk to you. If someone's exceptionally busy and really doesn't have time to speak with you in person, see if they'll talk over the phone.

After the Call

Take notes about how the call went. Did you make an appointment? Write it down in your calendar. Do you need to provide the person with a résumé, letter, or transcript? Did it go poorly? Are there any things you wish you'd said but didn't? Where did you get stuck in the conversation?

Now you know all about how to go about landing an interview. It's time to find out what to do once you've actually gotten one.

chapter 6

ACING THE INTERVIEW

Let's say you've booked six interviews, all with firms in which you're very interested. You're proud of yourself for getting the three on-campus interviews you bid for and for landing three additional appointments, one through a friend's employer, one from a company recruiter you met at a career fair, and one from a job listing you saw on Jobtrak. The hard part is over, and now you're ready to push the appointments back to the farthest corner of your mind, kind of like that corner of your closet where you last saw your interview suit. You've earned the right to be excited. But don't drop the ball!

This chapter aims to provide you with a more-or-less chronological, step-by-step description of things you can do to help make sure that the many interviews you've landed don't result in a stack of rejection letters. If you follow the advice outlined here, you should significantly improve your chances of interviewing successfully and finding yourself on the receiving end of that all-important job offer.

RESEARCH

When Interview Day rolls around and the interviewer asks you why you're interested in working for the company, your answer should *not* be: "Well, uh, I was hoping to learn more about your company today so I could address that very question." The time and place for that kind of question is the informational interview. On-campus interviews are interviews for jobs, interviews in which you will need to impress the recruiter with your understanding of the business, your enthusiasm for the specific position, and a well-thought out argument as to why you, specifically, are the best person for the job.

Read everything you can on the company prior to your interview. DO NOT show up for an interview unprepared! This is the most basic piece of advice we can give you; it's also the least heeded.

Depending on the size of the company, you'll find information either really easy or quite difficult to come by. Before you begin researching, spend a few minutes thinking about what you'd like to find out. You're looking for information on the job, the company, and the industry or field. More specifically, here are some things you might want to know:

Job-Related Information:
- Job requirements: the kind of skills you will need
- An idea of what the ideal candidate for the job would be like
- The kinds of growth opportunities that exist for you at this company
- Responsibilities of the job
- Training/management style
- Anything you can find out about your potential boss
- Salary and benefit standards for the industry (your career center might be able to provide some help here)

Company-Related Information:
- Size of company and location(s)
- Corporate structure of the company
- How the department you're interviewing with fits in with the rest of the company
- Ownership of the company—is it public or private, wholly owned or a subsidiary, or publicly traded on the stock exchange?
- Major products or services; what the company does
- Insight into the corporate culture
- Information on the mission of the company
- Plans for growth, expansion, or downsizing
- Anything about the president, CEO, or upper management that might shed light on the company culture or mission

Industry-Related Information:
- Recent mentions in the news
- Major developments among competitors
- A preliminary sense of the product or service and how it fits in with the competition (market share, pricing, and quality)

Sources

We suggest the following sources for your research:

Company Binders and/or Brochures in the Career Center

If you are unable to find anything on the company in the library, call it and request recruiting literature.

The Company's Web Site

An excellent resource for everything from product and service information to company structure and location.

Annual or Quarterly Reports

If the company is public, this financial information is available for anyone and, in larger companies' cases, you may even find it on the Web site.

Newspaper or Magazine Articles

If possible, do a Lexis/Nexis search of periodicals. Depending on the field or industry in which you're interested, there may be trade publications that are good places to start looking (for example, for software companies, you could check either *Wired* or *Macworld*).

Alumni Contacts

Check with the career center to see if any alumni listed themselves as contacts for that company. If so, give them a call, but be sure to explain how you got their name and why you're calling. Be sure to check with your own network of friends to find out if they know anyone who knows someone hired by the company. Talking with an employee may give you an inside glimpse into the culture and help answer some of your questions about its structure.

Informational Interviews

We mentioned informational interviews in the previous chapter as a way of getting your name and résumé out there. They are also a great way of learning about the company from an insider's perspective. You can learn about new developments or about one employee's opinion by asking questions such as: "Where do you see the company heading in the next year or so?" or "What do you like most about working here?" or "When you interviewed, what was it that made you want to work for this company?"

PRACTICAL DETAILS

All of the research and preparation in the world won't help you if you dress or behave inappropriately on the day of the interview. The little things discussed below may seem pretty basic, but that doesn't mean they aren't important. Remember that the interview gives you a very short time in which to make a big impression.

What to Wear

A Suit

You will need an interview suit, one that fits well and isn't too hot. We recommend a conservative black, navy, or dark grey suit for men as well as for women. Women tend to have more choice in color. It depends on with whom you're interviewing, but you can probably wear a teal, burgundy, red, or purple suit if you like.

The beauty of a more traditional color is that it will be acceptable everywhere, whereas if you go with something less traditional, you may end up having to purchase that basic black suit anyway.

The Other Side of the Table

If you're getting your suits dry-cleaned right before the interview, you might want to allow a slight cushion. One applicant missed his 9:00 A.M. on-campus interview with a *SCORE!* recruiter because his dry cleaner failed to show up at 7:30 A.M. as promised, leaving the applicant with nothing to wear.

A Shirt or Blouse

It's best to go with a white button-down shirt for men and a blouse for women, although men can certainly go with striped or solid color shirts. Men will need an undershirt, and women should think about camisoles if their blouses are at all sheer. Avoid wrinkled shirts, stained cuffs, or low-cut necklines. You're aiming for something simple that won't detract from the professional, collected appearance you're trying to convey.

Shoes

For men, standard dress shoes work well (loafers, wing tips, etcetera). Be sure to wear dark socks that match your shoes. Women should stick with heels that aren't too high. It's tough to focus all of your energy on the interview when part of you is afraid you'll break your neck if you tread carelessly. Women should not forget to bring along at least one extra pair of stockings or hose, in case of unsightly runs.

Ties

Men should keep their ties relatively subdued. This depends on the company, of course. For financial institutions or consulting firms, you may want to play it safe. Ties can, however, be good conversation pieces. Ties give men a bit of a creative outlet, but if you're inclined to make a statement, remember that you can wear that Mickey Mouse tie if you wish, but you might be talking with someone who hates Disney.

Accessories

Women should keep jewelry to a minimum; small earrings and a simple necklace are recommended. Anything larger is liable to detract from you and might jingle or clink. Men should avoid wearing earrings to interviews.

Dress Codes

71

Some companies have dress codes that can include policies on uniforms, nose rings or other jewelry, and appropriate hair styles for men and women. Not all companies have written dress codes, but it's possible that an unwritten code exists. Only you can decide if you're willing to let your appearance determine whether or not you get a job. If you wouldn't be comfortable working for a formal organization, you might want to research dress codes prior to the interview.

In general, the interview is a more formal situation than you'll find on the job. While nobody looks twice at earrings on men on campus, in an interview it's a different story.

The Recruiter's Attire

We've talked about your appearance; let's spend a minute on the recruiter. Companies expect their representatives to maintain a professional appearance and manner. While it's likely that your interviewer will be at least as formally dressed as you, there is a chance that she will be dressed more casually. Unless you've been given explicit directions otherwise, plan on wearing your suit. It's better to be over- rather than underdressed.

What to Bring With You

If you have a nice briefcase, you can use it, but it may not be necessary. You might be better off with a simple folder, something that has room for a pad of paper, a pen, and copies of your résumé and transcript, references, and letters of recommendation (if you wish to bring them). Check with the career center, company representative, or company literature to see what you'll be expected to bring. A pen and paper will come in handy if you need to take a few notes or refer back to your own list of questions to ask.

If you're coming from class, you may have a backpack, your normal clothes, a jacket, and any materials you brought for the interview. Try to avoid bringing all of that with you to the interview room. You should be able to leave these articles in the waiting area, or, perhaps, behind the counter at the career center.

Personal Appearance

Facial Hair

Men should avoid unusually large side burns, goatees, or any facial hair that might detract attention from their qualifications and on to their appearance. A well-trimmed beard or mustache shouldn't be a problem. If you don't wear a mustache or beard, make sure you shave before the interview. Stubble may be fine on *Party of Five*, but it looks sloppy in an interview.

Hair Styles

Conservative is the rule here. Men should avoid long hair. If you really can't cut your hair, then at least brush it back into a neat ponytail. Women should stick to simple styles that don't require a lot of tending. You never know when you'll need to walk two blocks to an office or across campus in a rainstorm. Pulling your hair back is always a good option, but be yourself. If you like to dye your hair, fine, but don't show up for an interview with purple hair. It doesn't give off the impression of someone who will represent a company well.

Grooming Tips

Women should feel fine wearing makeup, but don't overdo it. You're not getting ready for a night on the town. You'll probably be in a room with bright neon lighting, and heavy makeup will look out of place. Women should check to make sure their lipstick is not on their teeth and that their eye makeup isn't giving them dark smudges under their eyes.

It's not a bad idea to brush your teeth before an interview. Garlicky or oniony food can be overwhelming in such a small space. Checking for spinach or poppy seeds in your teeth isn't a bad idea, either.

If you have extremely long fingernails, think about trimming them before the interview. People will notice long nails and might wonder if you'll be spending time fretting over broken nails. If you chew your nails, people may take it as a sign of nervousness. Try not to.

If you want to have a mint or piece of gum before the interview, be sure to spit it out before you walk into the interview room.

Smell Good

Men and women should avoid strong aftershaves, cologne, or perfume. That room with the bright lighting is quite small, and you don't really want to fumigate your interviewer, do you? However, you will be nervous, dressed in a warm suit. So don't forget deodorant.

Your goal should be to be so well groomed that people will not notice your grooming. You don't want someone to focus on your hair or the wrinkles in your suit instead of on you.

The Countdown Begins: Making Your Way to the Interview Room

Once you're all decked out and ready to make a favorable impression on the interviewer, you'll have to actually get to the interview and behave in an appropriate manner in the presence of the interviewer.

Getting There

Some career centers will arrange for interviews through the on-campus interviewing program that take place outside of the career fair, either at a local hotel or another location on-campus (perhaps at the student union). If you have arranged a first-round interview with a company on your own, you may need to meet their representative off campus. Regardless of where the interview takes place, allow plenty of time to get there. Even crossing campus from your dorm to the career center may take a little longer than anticipated. If you're not sure how much time to allow, plan on getting there early and bring a book or some homework.

A Trial Run

If you want to be absolutely sure you make it to the interview on time, take a trial run sometime beforehand and time your walk or your drive (if your trial run takes place on a weekend or off hours, remember to account for rush hour or weekday traffic patterns).

When you schedule an appointment somewhere off campus, don't be afraid to ask for directions. If you're going to a part of town or to a city nearby that's unfamiliar, buy a map or ask a friend. It's also okay to ask how long the interview might take or if there's any convenient parking nearby. Definitely bring a handful of quarters in case you encounter parking meters.

When You Arrive

In general, you'll be expected to go to the interview desk and check in. You may also be asked to check your name off of the company's appointment list so that the interviewer knows if you've arrived. Your career center may have specific rules. Check with them.

The Waiting Room

We know you're nervous. That's understandable. And, if the interviewer's previous appointment runs late and you have to spend an extra few minutes watching the little hand make its way around the clock, you have even more time in which to be nervous. Bring reading material, check your teeth, or strike up a conversation with your roommate from freshman year who just walked by, but be ready to walk down the hall with your interviewer as soon as your name is called.

Because on-campus interviews are so short, you'll need to make the most of your time with the interviewer. If you become engrossed in a conversation with someone while you're waiting, that's not a problem. But once your interviewer shows up, don't make him or her wait for you to finish. By the same token, if you're there early, don't duck into the bathroom or disappear without checking with the career center staff; your interviewer might come out, call your name, wait, and make a note that you were late or a no-show.

Interviewers are given a stack of résumés a few weeks in advance (if you were preselected for an interview) or on the morning of the interviews (for open or bidding schedules). They may have been able to only glance at your résumé. When they walk into a waiting area, they're probably wondering which of the students waiting there fits the name on the résumé. If your name is particularly hard to pronounce or if you have a name that might not necessarily match your appearance, pay attention. You won't look all that eager if someone says your name three times (albeit incorrectly) before you respond.

Introductions

When your name is called, stand up, leave your things, and shake the recruiter's hand—firmly, directly, and quickly. You've heard it before, and it's true: First impressions are lasting ones. Limp handshakes, crushing grasps, or handshakes that last 40 seconds won't do a lot to make a good impression. Make eye contact with the recruiter and smile. As you walk down the hall, you may feel a moment of awkwardness; the halls are often too narrow to allow two people to walk side by side. Defer to the recruiter to see if you should proceed first or not.

The Interview Room

We're using the word *room* loosely. More like cubby hole or cubicle, these rooms usually have one desk with a chair on either side. The recruiter will probably take the seat facing the doorway, and you'll sit in the one with the back to the door. If you are in any doubt, watch which chair the recruiter sits in and take the other one.

You've arrived at the moment of truth. You're sitting in the interview room opposite the interviewer, and the interview is about to begin. What can you expect to happen now?

THE "SCREENING" INTERVIEW

In general, you can look at interviews as screening interviews or follow-up interviews. Companies holding interviews on campus are screening candidates to determine who will be asked back for more rounds of interviews, often held at the company's office. We'll talk more about follow-up interviews in chapter 7. For now, let's focus on first-round or "screening" interviews.

A typical on-campus screening interview may contain some of the following elements:

Warn-Up:
- Introductions
- A rapport-building question or two
- Setting expectations for the interview (goals, structure, etcetera)

Body of the Interview:
- Questions about past experience (work, academic, or extracurricular), usually based on your résumé

- Questions on scenarios (often used to forecast how you might handle certain situations that occur in the job for which you're interviewing)
- Inquiries about short-term and long-term goals
- Logistical questions

Wrap-Up:
- A chance for you to ask questions
- The next step in the process

Interview Styles

You've heard the horror stories about interviews in which recruiters interrogate candidates, put them on the defensive, and generally torment them to see how they react under pressure. While it's true that you will encounter people with different styles, interviewing doesn't need to be so pressure filled or tortuous.

The stress interview aside, here are some types of interviews you might encounter:

Prescripted Interviews

An interviewer asks a series of questions that were decided upon ahead of time, perhaps to predict how you might handle job-related situations. These questions are asked of every interviewee. You may be asked the same questions in a follow-up interview or in a written application.

Conversational Interviews

Here you're asked questions based on your résumé, perhaps probing areas in which you have less experience and skimming over areas of obvious expertise.

Adapt to the Situation

You should get an idea pretty early on of your interviewer's style. Once you've identified it, you may want to pitch your answers to that style. People often like to talk with candidates who remind them of themselves. Don't be fake and don't directly ape someone, but if you can try to emulate the interviewer's style to at least some extent, the conversation may flow better.

Case-Study Interviews

Most often used by consulting companies, the case study interview revolves around a particular case, some data, and a question that you are asked to solve. Whether you get the correct answer or not is less important than how you got there. The interviewer will be looking for people with problem-solving skills, analytical ability, and presentation skills. Visit your career center to see if they have examples of case studies and strategies for solving them.

Questions You May Have to Answer

Whatever the type of interview you encounter, you will probably be expected to answer a variety of questions over the course of the meeting. As you research the company with which you are interviewing, make sure you also prepare yourself to answer the following types of questions.

Rapport-Building Questions

These quick questions are meant to put you at your ease, and will probably have to do with an interest or activity mentioned on your résumé. Here are a couple of examples:

> "Hello, _____, it's a pleasure to meet you. Tell me, how did you first hear about our company?"

> "So you heard about us through Thomas Stanyan! What did Tom say that made you want to apply?"

Past Experience

Anything mentioned on your résumé is game. The best preparation? Study your résumé. Be prepared to answer anything about what's listed there. The point of these questions is to shed light on your past work experience, including the responsibilities you've had, how much you enjoyed them, and what you learned.

> "I notice that you returned to your job at Shell three summers in a row. You must have enjoyed working there. Tell me about the dif-

ferent jobs you held each summer and how your responsibilities changed."

"Can you give me an example of a time when you made a decision that didn't work out as you'd hoped? How would you do things differently now?"

"You handled a lot of the office manager's functions when you worked for the accounting firm. How do you feel about doing clerical work?"

Questions About Experiences Not on Your Résumé

Interviewers may look at your résumé, identify the areas in which you seem to be well qualified, and then spend more time probing the areas in which your qualifications are less obvious. Don't be surprised if the interviewer explores your willingness and motivation to take on work responsibilities that would be new to you.

"We spend a certain amount of time selling clients on our products and services. I don't see much evidence of sales on your résumé. How do you feel about sales?"

"We work with databases quite a bit and I don't see any experience listed on your résumé—have you ever worked with databases?"

"We're particularly interested in employees who have a high comfort level with speaking in front of groups. Public speaking seems to be something you haven't had much chance to do. Can you tell me about a time when you had to address a group of people? How did you feel about your performance?"

Self-Assessment and "Get to Know You Better" Questions

Sometimes a recruiter will ask you to evaluate your own experiences, skills, and weaknesses:

"I see you're from Florida. What brought you up to New England, and why did you decide to attend school here?"

"If you could do it all again, what would you major in and why?"

"Which three adjectives would you use to describe yourself?"

Performance and Predictive Questions

Interviewers often look for a candidate with specific, demonstrated skills or abilities. If your résumé doesn't indicate what they're looking for, you might find yourself answering hypothetical questions along the lines of "Let's say this happens . . . . What would you do?" The interviewer is giving you the chance to show how you might perform under circumstances that you might encounter on the job.

"Let's say we hire you and you're working with a team of people. You have a disagreement with the project manager, and you're pretty sure you're right. How would you handle that situation?"

"What would be the most difficult aspect for you in giving a presentation to your managers summarizing the results of your last project?"

"You have just finished a three-month assignment and are enjoying a sense of satisfaction over a job well done, until you notice that the front page story in the newspaper contradicts part of your findings. Do you bury the story or bring it to the attention of your manager?"

Questions About Your Goals

This may seem like a self-explanatory category, but it's surprising how many students don't have answers to some basic questions. You don't need to have planned every detail of your next 40 years, but you should have some ideas about where you'd like your future to take you. Goal-setting indicates forward thinking, a proactive attitude, and long-term planning.

"What kinds of skills do you hope to develop in this job?"

"Where do you see yourself in five years? Ten years?"

Logistical Questions

In addition to explaining your qualifications, interests, and abilities, you'll also need to let the interviewer know when and where you're available to work. This is one area in which students seem poorly prepared. So many other aspects of the interview process take precedence that people sometimes entirely forget about the details. Companies may have specific calendar needs; whether you're available in late June or you're willing to wait until December to begin could be reason enough for getting or not getting a job. As a general rule, the more flexible you are, the better. While it's tough to envision the specifics of "life after college," we have one word of advice for you: Try.

"Assuming that we were to hire you, when would you like to begin working full time? What's the earliest you could start if for some reason our need is urgent?"

"We've already filled all of our summer training slots. We are still considering applicants for a January start date. How does that sound?"

What Are All These Questions Really Asking?

All of these questions help the interviewer to determine the answers to questions like: Are you manageable? Will you lead others? Are you flexible? Will you be a pleasure or a pain to work with? Do you take feedback well? Are you a self-starter, or someone who requires supervision and prodding? Are you honest? What is your work ethic like? Will you remain with the company for a while or will you need to be replaced immediately?

A hiring decision can be a costly one. Employers need to consider such factors before deciding whether or not to invest in you.

What the Interviewer Wants to Know About You

- Do you have the skills to do the job?

- Will you add value to the organization?

- Will you fit in with the company culture?

- How do you compare to other applicants?

HOW SHOULD YOU RESPOND?

It's true that interviews are inherently stressful. What takes place during an interview isn't entirely out of your control; you're the one who decides how to answer the questions you're asked. One of the best ways to prepare for an interview is to decide what you want the interviewer to know about you. Before you run out to the bookstore to buy every book on interviewing that's ever been published and memorize all possible questions along with some well-rehearsed answers, stop and think for a minute. Unless you deliver those answers with enthusiasm and sincerity, you'll come off as canned and insincere.

Instead, why don't you sit down and think about *why* you want this job. Are you passionate about the possibility? Do you feel any enthusiasm at all? Use those feelings. A job interview is your chance to select a few critical moments, skills, or experiences that you absolutely must convey to the interviewer, and figure out how to package them to suit different questions. This is not to suggest that you dominate the whole meeting or that you refuse to answer the questions asked. Instead, create an arsenal of some really amazing points and be ready to use them when the opportunity arises.

Your Arsenal

At a minimum, your arsenal should include your qualities, your work experiences, and your accomplishments.

Qualities

Highlight qualities that make you an excellent employee. Are you well organized? Always on time? Do you have a strong work ethic? Are you one of those "I must see this project to the end if it kills me" kind of people? Do you thrive on public-speaking opportunities? Are you shy and quiet, but masterful with computers? Are you a natural at motivating others? Decide which of these qualities will make you an invaluable employee and jump at the chance to say so, giving examples to illustrate why.

Work Experiences

These should be experiences that tested your mettle. Were you given the chance in that internship last summer to work on a project that culminated in a new employee manual? When you worked as a T.A. for the Intro to Psych class, did you actually manage not to faint when you were unexpectedly told to lecture a class, and end up captivating the lecture hall? Did you discover a knack for cold-calling prospective new customers when you worked as a student fund-raiser, setting the record for most money brought in? And did you suck it up when the editor-in-chief for the paper quit suddenly, leaving you to manage all of the staff meetings and keep your advertising accounts happy? These are the experiences that go way beyond a bullet point on a résumé. If you don't elaborate, who will?

Accomplishments

In which accomplishments do you take the most pride? Did you lead your college soccer team to an unexpected, come-from-behind, victorious season? Did you survive for two months in Spain with nothing other than rudimentary Spanish and a sense of adventure, navigating through remote Basque villages and teeming coastal towns? Were you the first person to petition for an interdisciplinary major combining your interest in geography with your passion for sociology? Perhaps you spent a summer building latrines in Latin America, teaching English to immigrants, working on Wall Street, or fighting fires in the Idaho wilderness. How were these experiences important to you?

Selling Yourself

Whether it's consulting, marketing, banking, teaching, or retail management, you need sales skills both to do the job and to get the job in the first place. If the thought of sales makes you cringe or think, "I'm not a salesperson," think again. You are constantly selling your ideas, your

The Other Side of the Table

If nothing else, bring all of the energy and enthusiasm you can muster with you to the interview. While neither enthusiasm nor energy will make up for a lack of work experience or good grades, they certainly can't hurt. How you say something is sometimes as effective as what you say. If you're not genuinely enthusiastic and interested, don't try to fake it. Recruiters are very good at detecting insincerity.

outlook, your opinion, and at an interview, your ability to do a job. An interview is a sale: A product (you and your potential as an employee) is being considered by a potential buyer (the company's representative).

Your goal is to show the recruiter how you can meet his or her company's needs. You have 30 minutes in which to impress the recruiter with how talented, intelligent, enthusiastic, and competent you are. If you don't brag about yourself, who will? More often than not, first-round interviews are meant to weed out the definite "nos," to identify the absolute "yeses," and to select a few "maybes." You need to explain why you're a "yes!" candidate (or at least a "maybe" who's worth another look). Almost every question gives you the chance to create and bolster a certain image. When you write a résumé, you choose every word carefully, opting for active, strong words and phrases. The answers you provide in an interview setting shouldn't be any different.

The key to being an effective salesperson is to listen to your audience. Pay attention. See what it is that he wants, and provide it. But remember to be honest about what you can and cannot do. And don't get let your bragging get out of hand. There's a fine line between being confident and being arrogant. Arrogance will alienate, offend, and even amuse your interviewer. You want to be respected at work, not ridiculed.

Practice

If you feel more comfortable working all of this out on paper, go ahead. Get a piece of paper and a copy of your résumé. Start by writing down a description of the job for which you're interviewing, including any qualifications. Under each column, list all of the qualities, work experiences, or accomplishments that seem important to you. Go back and read the job description again. Which of the items on your list best illustrate why you'd be a good person to fill that job? Identify two or three in each category. You might even write a brief blurb on each, making sure to give an example.

Ready to practice? If you have a friend going through a job search, why not put yourselves through some mock interviews? Exchange résumés and practice asking questions about everything on your résumé. Have you ever seen a lawyer preparing a witness for the stand? The lawyer might coach the witness on how to appear sympathetic, handle being badgered, remain calm under pressure, and expect the unexpected. Between the two of you, try to come up with some challenging questions. Read your friend's résumé with a critical eye, looking for any obscure detail, and start probing. Some candidates are so unfamiliar with what's on their résumé that they freeze in interviews, able to talk only once they have a copy of their résumé in front of them. Don't let that be you.

Common Interview Pitfalls

Solid preparation isn't enough; you need to be effective when you meet with the interviewer one on one. Well-prepared, well-qualified candidates can crash and burn in interviews due to common, easily avoidable mistakes. Let's take a look at some of the unnecessary mistakes that you should avoid making in an interview situation.

Nervous Habits

Foot tappers, table drummers, knuckle crackers, and incessant nodders who must bob their heads at everything are frequently encountered by recruiters. Some people show their nervousness verbally. Ever counted how many times you say "um," "I don't know," "like," or other small phrases? The best way to prevent these tics from appearing in the interview is to get feedback from friends, identify what you do when you're nervous, and practice keeping it under control. For example, if you really feel the need to drum your fingers on the table, hold your hands clasped in your lap. It'll be tough, but it'll help.

The Stone Face

One of the worst side effects of nerves is that your natural enthusiasm may be dampened. Are you the type who gets more and more somber when you're under the gun? Do you speak in a monotone, losing all inflection in your voice? Nothing relaxes people more than a smile. Try to focus on smiling, raising your eyebrows, and using your face to show agreement, puzzlement, or interest. The interview is your opportunity to breathe life into your application and to bring personality to your résumé.

Bad Posture

If you're slumped in your chair, wrapped up in a pretzel, or hunched in on yourself, your body language and posture are sending out messages that you may not want to project. A person might get the impression, however subtly, that you're tired, defeated, insecure, or scared. If you carry yourself well, head high and shoulders back, you will be less inclined to fidget and you'll appear more confident.

Poor Eye Contact

It's amazing how many people answer a question while looking at the clock, the ceiling, at the view, or off into space. If you don't meet your interviewer's eyes, you might appear nervous, insecure, or secretive, while direct eye contact sends out the message that you're steady, open, and have nothing to hide. This is not to suggest that you pierce the person across the table with your steady stare. It's okay to look down or somewhere else if you're gathering your thoughts or listening intently. But be aware of where your eyes wander and of what message that sends.

Don't Come *Too* Early

It's always better to be early than late, but not too early. If you're an hour early, you won't score any points, and you might even be underfoot. If you're going to be that early, walk around the block, go to a cafe, or sit in the car instead. Try to arrive five to ten minutes in advance, but no more.

Showing Up at the Wrong Time

You should plan on getting to the career center at least ten minutes early, and anticipate that you may finish late. Interviewers are on very tight schedules; it's not uncommon for them to run a little late. There are usually short breaks scheduled between interviews, which makes it possible to keep a candidate for a few minutes beyond the allotted time.

Self-Criticism

This is different from self-critique. Don't turn to the interviewer after having babbled for five minutes and say "I'm stupid sometimes" or "You didn't really need to know that, did you?" You're nervous. You may say things you wish you hadn't. There's a better way to fix the problem. Stop and say, "I don't think I answered your question. Do you mind if I give it another try?" It's even okay to admit you're nervous, but don't harp on it. The interviewer's attention may shift from your qualifications to your inability to stay focused under pressure.

Too Little Information

Try to avoid answering "yes," "no," or "that's correct" to questions which were meant to get you to talk. If you are too brief, you may find yourself answering a string of follow-up questions. This is your chance to tell the interviewer about yourself, not a race to see how many questions you can answer in a 30-minute period.

A recruiter might appreciate an occasional "That's a good question. I'm not sure" to a fudged half-answer. But don't talk yourself out of a job because you don't have any answers.

Tangents

Don't wander off on five tangents before or after answering the question. Applicants sometimes give great answers, only to follow them by a four-minute monologue, winding down with a comment like: "I talk too much. What was the question?" If you find that you're dragging your answers out, try repeating a question back to an interviewer or pausing for a moment to frame your answer in your head.

Poor Listening Skills

Listening skills may be as important as presentation, analytical, or problem solving skills to your interviewer—especially if you're considering a job with high client contact. If you aren't sure you understand a question, ask for clarification. If you're not sure you've answered something satisfactorily, ask.

Poor Observation Skills

You probably feel like you're about to be put under the microscope, subject to intense scrutiny, right? In a sense, you are. But don't get so caught up in how to answer the questions that you fail to notice how your answers are received. Make an effort to observe the interviewer's body language. Some interviewers will use subtle cues to lead a candidate to elaborate on or to cut short a point. You'll need to be observant to see if you've lost your interviewer's attention.

Lack of Professionalism

This is a vague term, but in this context it means that you should be polite, courteous, attentive, and try not to mention personal issues. The goal of the interview is to decide if you'll be coming back for another interview. Unprofessional behavior won't help. You might also think about your vocabulary. Try not to use *cool, awesome, like,* or other words that may work well in other contexts. Don't stretch for big vocabulary words whose meanings aren't totally clear to you. Using a word in an incorrect way is not a good way to impress a possible employer with your extensive vocabulary.

Pushiness

It's a good idea to be in control of yourself, but you don't want to immediately sit down and grill the interviewer with questions. If you dominate the meeting, you'll give off the impression of being pushy, not to mention that you could be sabotaging your chances at a second interview. If an interviewer isn't able to gather all of the data necessary to make a good decision, it's your loss.

Great Rapport, Poor Fit

Just because you and the interviewer seem to be thick as thieves, getting along beautifully, and discovering all sorts of common interests and experiences, this doesn't mean that you're doing your job—selling the interviewer on your qualifications.

The Wrong Right Answer

You're wrapped up in the moment, your adrenaline is pumping, you've developed a strong rapport with your interviewer, and then the question "This position requires extensive travel—how does that sound to you?" comes along. You ignore your fear of planes and say, "Great! I love to fly!" only to find yourself in three months clutching an airsick bag and cursing the day you ever wanted to be a business person. Sound overly dramatic? Maybe so, but it's not that hard to convince yourself that you can learn to like something, especially if it means you'll get a job. It's tempting. But be careful: You don't want to be stuck in a job that doesn't suit you.

Honesty Is the Only Policy

In an interview situation, you will feel pressure. People respond to pressure differently. Some would rather be struck down by lightning than have to say "no" to a question. If you don't have experience in something and you've been asked a direct question, say so.

Explain Your Deficiencies

In one interview, an applicant pinned a note of explanation to her transcript to explain a particularly brutal set of grades. Her father had been critically injured in a car accident that year and she missed most of the term. She acknowledged that for the next two quarters her grades continued to be affected, but that in her last two years she maintained a "B" average. A sad story, but it anticipated any questions the recruiter might have had.

There are different ways of saying no. You can say "no, never" and leave it at that, or you can say: "No, I haven't, but that's precisely why I'd love this job. I have done these two things which are directly related to this position, but I'm really interested in trying my hand at this. I think I'd be good at it because . . . ."

Resist the temptation to lie or misrepresent yourself. It's unethical, and it's not smart. It's hard enough to keep track of answers you've given when you're telling the truth; imagine how tough it will be to keep your story straight if it's based on a lie. If you decide to embellish, remember that interviewers often take notes, notes which are passed along with your file to subsequent interviews. You may not recall exactly what you said, but the interviewer could have it in black and white. And, as with your résumé, anything you say in an interview is fair game for verification.

WHAT YOU CAN EXPECT FROM YOUR INTERVIEWER

Don't forget that you are never totally at the mercy of your interviewer. There are certain standards of behavior that your interviewer is expected to maintain, including the following:

Courteous, Professional Behavior

Representatives of the companies recruiting on campus should be familiar with the policies of your career center. If you encounter questions that seem inappropriate, or any other behavior that isn't professional, talk to the career center staff or the coordinator of the on-campus interviewing program. Interviewers expect appropriate behavior from you; why should you expect any less from them?

Interviewers will be asking questions, taking notes, deciding what to ask next while they're listening to your answer and considering something you said five minutes ago, blocking out the muted conversations coming from the other interview rooms, scanning three résumés at once, picking up on what questions to ask which candidates, and facing a day with as many as 13 back-to-back interviews. An interviewer needs concentration and practice to interview smoothly.

The Interviewer From Hell

Most interviewers will keep the mood upbeat. It's possible, however, that you'll interview with someone and have a less than pleasant experience. Before you throw in the towel, keep in mind that it may be the day before your interviewer is retiring or leaving the company and the ill will or negative impressions you pick up may have nothing to do with you at all.

What we're getting at is that interviewers are not ogres put on earth to create misery and terror among college seniors. They're doing their job—finding strong enough candidates to pass to the second round.

Answers to Your Questions

Keep in mind that the interviewer is not the only person permitted to ask questions in this situation. Remember that research you did? Let's go back to that list of things you might want to know before going in to the interview. You should have found answers to a number of these questions already. If you haven't, here's your chance to learn more. Why not use this opportunity to find out about the company from an employee's perspective? Ask about the recruiter's experiences with the company.

- From your vantage point, what's a typical day like for someone in the position we're discussing?
- What do you like most about the company? The least?
- What brought you to Acme Corp.? Tell me about your experiences.
- You've probably seen people hired to do the job we're discussing. In your opinion, what do they find most/least challenging about the position?
- If you could change one thing about Acme, what would it be?

However, keep in mind that you need to tread carefully when asking questions. You don't want to take over the interview or turn off the interviewer. If the opportunity presents itself, ask one or two questions at the end of the meeting. If that's not possible due to time constraints, get a business card and ask if you can follow up over the phone or via e-mail.

An Indication of What the Next Step Is

If the recruiter hasn't mentioned what the next step in the process is or when you can expect to hear an answer, go ahead and ask! You have every right to know.

ENDING ON A POSITIVE NOTE

The interviewer winds things up by thanking you for your time. What do you do? Remember to shake hands, thank the person, and ask what the next step is or when you can expect to hear something. It's also acceptable to ask for a business card. If your interviewer doesn't have one, the career center should have all the necessary contact information.

Regardless of how long or short the interview was, how well you hit it off with your interviewer, or how successfully you think you presented your case, treat your interviewer with courtesy. Don't burn any bridges needlessly. Try to end the interview on a strong note.

chapter 7

AFTER THE INTERVIEW

Congratulations! You made it through the interview without any permanent damage. Now that your heart has stopped racing and you've hung up your suit, why not sit down and do a little evaluating? How did it go? Were there any questions that stumped you or made you feel uncomfortable? Anything that strikes you as particularly in your favor? It's a good idea to write down your impressions immediately after the interview, for three reasons:

- To have a record in case you continue talks with the company
- To improve your interviewing skills
- To review the answers you gave and see if you need to clarify any points

Let's talk about that last reason for a moment. If you feel strongly enough that you need to set the record straight, either because of an incomplete answer you gave or because you've had time to further consider your ability to meet the company's needs, go ahead and do it. But don't expect too much. Depending on the interview process, the decision may or may not have already been made.

THANK-YOUS

Thanking an interviewer for his time isn't something that you do every once in a while, if you feel particularly excited about an interview. It's a necessary courtesy. You're not finished until you send this note.

Who Gets Them

For a first-round interview, you should thank anyone with whom you interviewed. These interviews usually take place with one interviewer, but if you speak with two people, thank them both. If you have contact information for only one person, mention the other in the letter.

If you go to later rounds in the process, you'll want to send thank-yous to the people you meet there as well. If you meet someone for only two minutes, you don't necessarily need to send a letter directly to him, but be sure to mention his name when you thank the person with whom you spent the most time.

What to Say

Thank-you letters shouldn't be cause for too much concern. The important thing is to send them promptly. It's a good idea to thank the person for her time, restate how interested you are in the opportunity, and clarify any confusing points from the interview.

To Type or Not to Type

Handwritten thank-you notes are perfectly acceptable, as long as they're legible. If you're unsure, or if your writing is indecipherable, type the letter. Using stationery that matches your résumé and cover letter is fine. If you really like thank-you cards, you can send them. Avoid getting too casual. We recommend staying away from anything frilly or humorous. It's not that recruiters don't have a sense of humor, but what's funny to you could be offensive to someone else. You never know.

What to Include

For the most part, sending a note is all you need to do. But there are two instances in which you might include other items. First, if the employer asks you for references, transcripts, or other materials that you don't have at the interview, sending them with a thank-you note is a prompt way of getting everything in. The other reason might be because you find an article in the paper or a magazine the next morning that reaffirms something covered in your interview. While the whole brownnosing rule still applies (as in, nobody likes one), if you see something that is genuinely relevant, it can't hurt to send it in.

Other Ways of Saying Thanks

Faxes, e-mails, and voicemail messages may also be used to say thanks. We still prefer to receive thank-you cards in the mail, but faxes and e-mails are almost as good. Leaving a voice mail, however, isn't really an acceptable form of expressing your appreciation.

THE WAITING GAME

You've made it through the first hoop. You have questions about how you did, about the benefits of the job (on the off chance you get it), and about what to expect next. You want to know more specifics about reporting relationships, about possible placement, and a hundred other things whirling around in your mind. And more than anything, you just want to sit down and talk to someone who was in your shoes a year ago, someone who made the transition from college to the working world and who might be able to give you some insight. What do you do?

You can certainly contact the interviewer with follow-up questions, but remember that he may be incredibly busy. Just as you should tread carefully when posing your own questions during the interview, you should try to avoid harassing your interviewer in the weeks following the interview. Also, depending on where your application is in the decision process, any interactions you have with the company may contribute to the overall impression you make. Do you want to appear overly anxious? High maintenance? Respectful of the company's time? The best thing you can do right now is to wait.

Chances are that when you last spoke with a company rep, she or he gave you a time frame, anywhere from "we'll call you by the twenty-first" to "we'll get back to

Don't Badger the Interviewer!

Whatever you do, don't badger the interviewer, however many questions you might have. For all you know, you're in the "maybe" pile, and one phone call too many could tip the scales in the wrong direction.

you as soon as we can, but it can take a few weeks." You have to decide how long you can hold out before calling, but calling before the date you've been given isn't a good idea. People are busy, more than one person may be involved in the selection process, and hiring decisions often take longer than anticipated. It's hard to remember this, but while you may be checking your voicemail every half hour in the hope that a company calls you, they could be looking at hundreds of applications, all requiring consideration and follow-up.

The only reason for calling prior to a deadline is if something changes in your status. For example, if you've been talking to two companies simultaneously, and Company B offers you a job but you're more interested in Company A, then you'd better call Company A and let the recruiter know what's going on. Don't try to be clever and pretend you have another offer just to get an answer. It's unethical, and whenever you lie, there's a chance that people might find out.

Sound Professional

If you're waiting to hear back from companies regarding jobs, you might want to rethink your answering machine message. If you really must have music, conversations, monologues, or political statements, at least state your name and your number. Your friends will still think you're cool if you revert to the old "Hi, this is Jonathan Miller at 555-3333. I'm sorry I missed your call, but if you leave a message, I'll call you back as soon as I can." And if they tease you, just remember you'll laugh last, once you're employed.

96

While you should make every effort to find out what to expect, it is possible that you left the interview without asking about the next step. In this case, you have the right to call and ask about when you can expect to hear an answer. Let's say that you do ask, only to be told you'll hear in a few days or something equally vague. We suggest waiting two weeks from your interview date. At that point it's fair to call and inquire as politely as you can about your application. You should get one of three answers: they're sorry, but they can't offer you another interview; they'd like you to come in for a second round; or they haven't made a decision yet. If you get the last response, ask for a more definite decision deadline.

REJECTION

The call or the letter finally comes, the one you're waiting for: "We appreciate your time, but aren't able to offer you a second interview." While a letter may seem impersonal to you, many companies save time by sending rejections out in the mail rather than calling people directly. If you make it to a second or even subsequent rounds of interviews, you might get a phone call rather than a letter.

Following Up

Nobody likes to be rejected. You're probably upset, and you should be, if this was an opportunity in which you were genuinely interested and for which you had done some research. But be honest: If you didn't do your homework prior to the meeting, certain that your charisma and charm would carry you through, then you might want to think less about how unfair it is and more about what you can do to improve. And then there are those occasions when—while you fit in well with the culture and got along beautifully with the recruiter—you just don't have the technical skills or experience necessary for the job.

If, on the other hand, you were just interviewing to get practice, or if you decided after learning more about the job that it wasn't for you, you can examine your own performance to see how you could do a better job in the future.

Getting Feedback

You've probably heard that it's a good idea to get feedback from interviewers so that you can learn from your experiences. If you're planning on calling the recruiter to ask for suggestions on what you could do differently, remember that recruiters are busy, nobody likes to have to reject people, and some companies even have policies of not discussing the specifics of an application. Company policies differ, and so will a recruiter's willingness to help you. If you'd like to try to get feedback but don't relish the thought of getting another rejection over the phone, you can e-mail your questions (a good technique if you're having trouble reaching the recruiter over the phone).

No Means No, Doesn't It?

If you were rejected, it's more than likely that you didn't have the right qualifications, experience, or fit; still, there is a slight chance that you were close. How you handle the rejection might be enough to make you stand out as a future possibility. It's unlikely, but possibly worth your time. We suggest that you write a quick letter thanking the recruiter for his or her time and stating your disappointment and continued interest in the company. You'll need to focus on other companies in your search, but at least you'll have the satisfaction of knowing that you tried.

SUBSEQUENT ROUNDS OF INTERVIEWS

Let's say you get the call that says, "We were impressed with your application, and we'd really like you to come in for another round of interviews." After you get off the phone and finish doing your victory dance, you'll need to prepare. It's not time to relax yet; you still need to make a good impression on a new group of interviewers before the offer is yours.

Answers to Some Questions You Might Have

What Is a Round, Exactly?

Interviews are set up to qualify or disqualify someone for the next round of competition. If you're asked back for a second round, you've made it to the next level.

How Many Rounds Are There?

As many as the company says there are. Not a satisfactory answer, we know, but the number of steps in an interview process is up to each company. Three or four rounds of interviews seem pretty standard, but don't be surprised if you're called back for more or less than that. The best thing you can do for yourself is to ask the recruiter what the interview process looks like.

How Much Research is Necessary?

You'll want to delve even deeper into the company's structure, history, and products or services. If you've already gathered information on them, but figured you wouldn't waste your time assimilating it unless you made the cut, then now is the time to do so. The people with whom you interview will expect a certain familiarity with their company. Make sure you're prepared.

What Should I Wear?

Play it safe and dress conservatively unless the recruiter specifically tells you otherwise. It's always better in an interview situation to be over- rather than underdressed.

What Should I Bring?

You may be meeting quite a few people, and you'll want to jot down names, titles, etcetera. In addition, you may be learning more about the job's requirements, hours, and benefits, information that you should write down. Bring paper, bring pens, and by all means take along copies of your résumé and transcripts. Ask the company representative if there's anything else you can provide.

Where Should I Go?

In general, second rounds are held at a local company office, at a hotel near your campus, or, occasionally, at the company's offices in another city. They might even be over the phone. You'll need to find out where the interview is, when it's taking place, and what the best way is to get there. Ask for directions if you need them.

What Questions Should I Ask?

Make a list of questions and be sure to get them answered. Again, make sure you've read all materials provided by the company and that you've done enough research. You don't want to look foolish by asking a question that would have been easily answered if you had read page 3 of the company's recruiting brochure.

How Much Will I Make?

One way of broaching this sensitive subject is to ask about the benefits package. That way, you may get salary information as well as other benefits offered by the employer.

Should I Ask About Salary?

It's usually considered polite to wait for the company representatives to bring up money. We'd suggest that you hold off on asking about salary and wait to see if you get called in for another round. You should, however, have an answer ready if the company asks you about your salary requirements. It's common to give a range of figures (we'll talk more about this in chapter 9, "Weighing Your Options").

What About Travel Reimbursement?

Depending on how large the recruiting budget is, companies may offer to pay all or part of your expenses if you're traveling some distance to interview with them. The larger, more established the company, the greater the chance is that the company will pick up the tab. But before you think you've scored a free trip with a room at the Hilton, you should ask. Some companies can't afford to do that and will offer to reimburse you for a lump sum of money. If that's the case, you'll need to hold on to receipts you incur and find out to whom to send them.

What Will the Format of the Interview Be?

Second and other subsequent rounds will differ. Your day could include a tour, a meal, a group interview (the "group" may mean a group of candidates or a group of company representatives—if you're not sure, ask), or an informal social gathering with potential future colleagues. You may encounter written applications, written tests (on anything from analytical, problem-solving, or writing skills), or even assessment exams determining your "fit" with the other employees. As you make your way further into the interview process, you may find more efforts on the company's part to provide you with information.

Who Will Interview Me?

First rounds are usually held by company recruiters or employees who are recent alumni of your college. Occasionally, you might interview with a potential manager in a first round. In later rounds, you may or may not see the company recruiter again. You will probably meet employees currently in the job for which you're being interviewed, mid- to upper-level managers, your potential boss, and senior managers or officers. The company's size, location, and overall budget for recruiting will partly determine with whom you meet.

How Do I Prepare for a Phone Interview?

Some companies will set up next-round interviews over the phone or even by video conferencing. Preparing for a phone interview should be similar to what you'd do for a face-to-face interview, but remember the following tips: You won't be able to gauge your interviewer's reactions to you as easily as in a face-to-face interview; nor will she be able to read you. Put as much inflection into your voice as possible. Smile often even though nobody can see you. Convey enthusiasm and energy over the phone. As we've mentioned before, don't rustle papers or chew gum. If you have call waiting, ignore it! Whoever it is will call you back if it's important.

Accommodate Yourself

When you make the arrangements for a phone interview, be accommodating about times and dates. But remember to take your own circumstances into account. If your interviewer suggests a time when you know that your roommates will be home and waiting to use the phone, or if you're going to be at work and won't have a private line, try to propose an alternative time.

If You Don't Know, Ask

For every rule, there's an exception. We can't emphasize enough that the process you go through will depend on the company. Don't be surprised if some small companies send their president or the newest employee and, when asked about the interview "process," look surprised. It's possible that they may be making it up as they go along. Other large companies may have the recruiting process down to a science, complete with seven steps that were hammered out years ago. Then again, you might find the small company with everything carefully orchestrated and the large company with no idea of how to process applicants. The best way to understand what you're in for is to ask. You can ask the career center or any friends who interviewed with the company in previous years or during earlier recruiting seasons. You can also ask the recruiter.

You may be rejected at any point during the process. If you fail to hear back from the company after any round, give them a call. It's painful to make the phone call, especially if you're already sure of the outcome, but you deserve to get an answer. If you are met with nothing but good news, on the other hand, you will need to think about what to do if you're extended an offer of employment. The final section of this book will lead you through that process.

section **3**

THE OFFER

chapter 8

THE OFFER COMES IN

You've bought the suit, polished the shoes, tweaked your résumé a million times, and sat through more interviews than you care to think about. You've been so gracious, engaging, confident, eloquent, and charming that even you are tired of hearing yourself talk. You may have been rejected once or twice, a pride-pricking experience that is never any fun. And perhaps, on occasion, you've found yourself rubbing sore feet after yet another interview and wishing you'd applied to grad school or decided to teach overseas—anything to avoid facing the void after commencement. You're so sick of waiting for your phone to ring that you're just about ready to chuck it out the window. You wonder how long these people are going to take to make a decision—after all, it's your life that's hanging in the balance. But then it happens. You hear what you've been waiting for all along: They want you.

THE OFFER

Getting a job offer is kind of like buying a car. You can get so wrapped up in the emotion of it that you forget to check the car for an owner's manual, a spare tire, loose belts, or chips in the paint. You might skip pricing the model of your choice at other dealerships. All you can think about is how amazing it feels to drive a new car. It's the same thing with a job offer. It's much more fun to picture an office with a view and a steady paycheck than it is to pay attention to details.

Some Things to Keep in Mind When You're Receiving an Offer

Ask Questions

Don't be shy about asking questions at this stage of the process. The company representative has decided that you are the candidate she wants, and she should be more than willing to accommodate you. If any part of the offer doesn't make sense to you or if you feel you misunderstood a point, ask the company representative to go over it again. This is your chance to get as many details as you can. If you're unclear on something but would prefer not to bring it up with your potential employer, why not discuss the details of the offer with family or friends? Find out what's "standard," either for your industry or your experience level. You can also go to the career center and speak with someone there.

Salary

If salary hasn't been mentioned by either side yet, you *must* ask about salary and benefits now. While it's never easy to bring up the issue of compensation, you need to know all of the facts before you can make an informed decision. It won't get any easier to ask the hard questions once you've agreed to work for the company.

Think Before You Commit

To a certain extent, the company representative is trying to sell you on working for his company. Don't let yourself be convinced to gloss over any points that are important to you. Don't commit to anything immediately! Even if you're absolutely certain, ask for a day to think things over. That way you won't agree to something in the heat of the moment only to realize that there's a problem that precludes you from doing a good job.

Say Thanks

Be sure to thank the person for the offer. Be as polite as you can—you're setting the tone for future interactions with the company.

The process of extending an offer differs by company. Once your potential employer has made the decision, a representative—perhaps your future boss, someone in management, or one of your interviewers—will contact you. You'll either be asked to come in person or you'll receive an offer of employment over the phone. The offer itself could be as casual as a question asking you whether or not you're ready to come on board, or as formal as requiring you to read through an employee contract and sign on all of the dotted lines. More than likely you'll find something in between—a verbal question, followed by an offer letter requiring you to sign and return it, along with any other documents you might need (such as an employee handbook, health care info, company policies, etcetera).

In the pages to come, we're going to spend some time going over the benefits, the rewards, and some details that might be included in your offer.

A Typical Offer

Whether it's over lunch or over the phone, expect your offer conversation to go something like this:

- Congratulations from the company representative

- A discussion of the offer (benefits, rewards, and details)

- Closing the deal: Are you ready to commit? If not, when will you be? Setting a deadline

- A chance for you to ask questions, follow-up talks arranged

THE BENEFITS

No offer is complete without a summary of the package of benefits you will be eligible to receive. Your future employer will most likely wish to take you through them. A benefits package can be very basic or more complicated. Here's a look at possible benefits a company might offer:

401K or Other Retirement/Pension Plans

A typical 401K plan allows you to contribute up to a certain percentage of your salary each year to a retirement fund. These plans allow you to save for retirement without having to pay tax on the money you invest or the interest you accrue until you actually use the money (if you withdraw money early, you will pay penalties). A few companies will even match employee contributions.

Bonus Potential/Schedule

Employees often earn bonuses (quarterly, semiannually, or annually) in addition to their base salary. Bonuses are usually tied to performance measurements: The better you or the company performs, the higher your bonus. When discussing compensation, make sure you're clear on how bonuses are determined and how your salary breaks down (what base you can count on, what your bonus range is, and how common it is for people to earn maximum bonuses).

Company Car and/or Expense Account

If your job requires an extensive amount of driving or a lot of client contact, you may be given the use of a company car and/or an expense account. You'll be expected to provide details about the mileage as well as receipts and allocations for any company-related expenses.

Health Insurance

The larger the company, the better your chances are of getting broad coverage. Here are some of the possible forms health benefits can take:

Medical Insurance

If your company provides Health Maintenance Organization (HMO) or Point of Service (POS) coverage, you'll need to select a primary care physician who either treats you or refers you to other doctors in his/her medical group. You may be covered for a physical once every year or two along with most doctor visits and prescriptions for medication. In general, you will pay a "co-payment" when you visit the doctor or fill out a prescription ($10–20 is common).

Be sure to ask the following questions: How high is the deductible? How much money will be deducted from your paycheck every month? How much is the employee contribution? Ask to see a copy of your company's plan for specifics.

Other Insurance

Once again, the larger the company, the more likely you are to be covered for more than your basic medical needs. Dental or eye care is rarely covered by smaller organizations. If your potential employer does provide dental benefits, the coverage could vary from comprehensive dental care to reimbursement for up to a specific dollar amount per year. If eye care is covered, you may be able to get a new pair of glasses or contact lenses in addition to regular eye exams each year. If you are eligible to receive some form of dental or eye care, find out what the deductible is. If you're interested in alternative forms of medicine (i.e., massage therapy, psychoanalysis, acupuncture, chiropractic care, etcetera), you should ask to see a copy of the company's policy; it should explain whether or not such forms of medicine are covered in detail.

Other Perks

Companies sometimes go to great lengths to provide employees with less conventional benefits, benefits that set them apart. Some of these benefits might include discounts at health clubs or a "health allowance," money that may be used for gym memberships or health-related classes; complimentary sodas or coffee; snacks or merchandise from accounts; occasional tickets to sporting events; discounted tickets to concerts, performances, etcetera; free movie screenings; memberships at wholesale warehouse stores, and so forth. These perks are often industry-related and will depend on who your clients are, where your company is located, and what you specialize in. Some companies—particularly those in sales—will also encourage employees to achieve goals by offering free trips, dinners out on the town, or gift certificates to local stores.

109

Paid Holidays

There's a difference between vacation and paid holidays. Paid holidays are days that you get off in addition to your vacation. Which holidays you're given will depend on your employer. Certain days—Labor Day, Thanksgiving, Christmas, New Year's Day, Memorial Day, and the Fourth of July—are standard, paid holidays. Other holidays such as Veterans Day, Columbus Day, and Martin Luther King Jr. Day may not be holidays for your company. Sometimes companies will close their doors for additional days such as the Friday after Thanksgiving, but not always. If you're going into retail, you will definitely want to ask about this, because some of your busiest work days will be on the holidays that everyone else has off.

Profit Sharing

Some compensation plans include profit sharing. If you are eligible, you will receive a small share of the company profits. You might get a check monthly, quarterly, or annually, depending on your company's plan, and on how big company profits are during a particular period.

Referral Bonuses

You might be given cash incentives if you refer friends to work for the company. These bonuses are sometimes paid after the new employee has hit a three-month mark, to protect the company from an employee who refers a bunch of people who aren't serious about the job. Some companies offer movie tickets, weekend getaways, or other fun bonuses.

Retreats or Conferences

Retreats allow for companies to provide training for new and existing employees, to work on building rapport and team spirit, and to allow for a little fun on the job as well. Retreats may be specifically for training, for setting revenue or performance goals, for reviewing mission statements, or for meeting with and learning from other people in the industry. The range is huge.

Overtime Pay

If it's important to you to be compensated for all the hours you put in on the job, make sure you will be paid for overtime. One way to find this out is to directly ask your employer. Another way is to determine whether your job is classified as an "exempt" or a "non-exempt" position. Exempt positions usually involve some form of decision-making or managerial responsibility, while non-exempt jobs do not. If your job is classified as exempt, you will probably not be able to receive overtime pay.

Salary

You will receive wages for the job you do. Most full-time employees are paid a salary rather than an hourly wage. This means you'll be paid a lump sump each pay period. Certain jobs will offer overtime or allow you to rack up the hours you work beyond the normal 40 to apply towards vacation days. If you are discussing a salaried position, you should ask about typical work weeks (how many hours a week, the hours you should expect to be in the office) as well as about overtime pay.

If you're taking a sales job, you may be paid on commission. This means that you'll be paid for every sale you bring in, whether it's a percentage of the sale or a fixed amount of money. Employees on commission may sometimes receive a minimum monthly salary. You may also get a "draw" during training or slow months. A draw is a set amount of money that the company will pay you with the understanding that you will soon be selling enough to generate your own salary. Some employers will give you a draw for a set number of months or ask you to consider the draw a loan from your future earnings (in other words, you'll need to pay it back).

Scholarships

Some companies will help employees pay for graduate school. Scholarship money may be based on your tenure with the company. Companies may put some restrictions on the scholarship, such as imposing a time limit on how long you can wait after leaving the company to enroll in school, asking you to work part time and go to school part time, or to commit to returning to the company once you finish school.

Sick Days

Some companies will give employees a certain number of sick days per year. Sick days are pretty self-explanatory: If you're sick, you may take a day that won't count as a vacation day. You're usually limited in the number of sick days you may use a year, and companies may require notes from your doctor for extended absences.

Signing Bonus

A signing bonus is exactly what it sounds like—a bonus that is given to you when you sign an offer letter. Think about the baseball draft. College students won't attract the same lucrative offers as professional athletes, but the principle remains the same. Companies offering a one-time bonus up front can make an overall package look better without having to commit to a higher salary.

Stock Options

Rapidly-growing, start-up companies that have yet to go public sometimes give employees stock options. Stock options work a little like

Profit Without Risk

Another nice benefit of options is that you don't have to invest any of your money until you know it's a safe investment. Let's say you're given 1,000 options at $1.00 a share, only to watch the stock go down to $.01 a share. If you'd had to purchase the shares rather than hold on to the option to buy, you would have paid $1,000 for stock that's now worth $10.

shares of stock. The difference is that while stock options reserve you the right to exercise (or buy) your options, they aren't the same as owning stock itself. The beauty of stock options is that you can buy your options at a set price regardless of how much the stock is actually worth. Here's an example: You're given 1,000 stock options with a price of $1.00 a share. If the value of the stock goes up to $100 a share in five years, you will only have to pay $1,000 for stock that's worth $100,000. That's a tidy profit.

Because stock options usually have vesting periods—the amount of time you must remain with the company before being able to exercise them—they're also good tools for retaining valuable employees.

Stock Purchase Plan

Giving employees of publicly-traded companies the chance to purchase stock in the company with pre-tax earnings, at a slightly discounted rate, or automatically, is a nice incentive. This works well because employees who own stock in the company will be more inclined to work hard.

Tuition Reimbursement

Some companies will reimburse employees for self-development or continuing education classes. You may need to show proof of enrollment or registration.

Vacation

This aspect of your benefits package is often related to tenure with the company (the longer you've been there, the more vacation you get). Typical offers give new employees one or two weeks a year. Some companies give you an extra week after two years; other firms will wait five years. In general, companies have rules about using vacation days before you earn them, and they generally encourage employees to take time off at the end of December.

THE REWARDS

Your potential employers are keenly interested in painting as favorable a picture of the company as possible. With that in mind, they may wish to highlight the ways you will be rewarded in addition to the benefits we just discussed. We've already discussed compensation and benefits. The following is a list of potential nonmonetary rewards of a job. Even if none of these factors is brought into the discussion, you should at least begin to identify those which are most important to you. As a new entrant into the job market, you might want to make the most of opportunities that will teach you something—opportunities providing training, skill development, and professional growth.

Challenge

If you have a company car, a huge expense account, and a job that uses about four percent of your brain, you may find yourself climbing the walls. Then again, if you go with the brand new business that requires super-human commitment and the ability to wear twelve hats at once, will you be worn out within three months? It's not easy to gauge how challenging a particular job will be until you do it. People require a varying degree of challenge in their work. How important is this to you?

Community Involvement

If community involvement is a high priority, you can certainly volunteer on your own time. You might also pay attention to opportunities supported by your future employer. Some companies sponsor corporate volunteer programs—perhaps as a Big Brother or Big Sister, as a tutor, or as a volunteer for an environmental organization or a soup kitchen.

Company Culture

Company culture is hard to nail down. You have to think about the office environment—and we don't mean warm temperatures, spacious offices, or breathtaking views. What's the office climate like? Are people psyched to be there? Is there a sense of teamwork? Do employees feel appreciated? Do they take pride in their work? Do people wear roller-blades in the lunch room? Is there a high turnover rate among employees, or do people remain for a long time? Can you envision yourself flourishing in and contributing to the company?

Company Mission

If company culture helps capture how a company does business, the company's mission statement should provide insight into why the company does what it does. Why are employees excited about the company and the direction in which it is headed? And if they're not, why not? The final question you need to ask is of yourself: How important is it to work for a company with established goals, a sense of purpose, and a mission?

Fun

Why are you thinking about fun when we're talking about work? The two ideas aren't necessarily mutually exclusive. Your colleagues, the office atmosphere, the work you do—all contribute to how much fun you have, how productive you are, and how rewarded you feel at the office. While your idea of heaven may be to see colleagues during the work week only, you may wish for a more social atmosphere, one in which any company training sessions, retreats, or holiday parties are not only well attended, but actually enjoyable. If you're curious about the extent to which people socialize at work, you should ask. You might also inquire about retreats, sports activities (some companies have teams competing in various citywide recreation leagues), or voluntary social events outside the office.

Great Colleagues

The people with whom you interact on a daily basis will play a large part in your job satisfaction. Pay careful attention to all of the people with whom you've interacted throughout the interview process. Think about any indications you've seen to help you understand if you'll be excited to work with your potential colleagues. You should also give some thought to how important it is to you to have colleagues in the first place, especially if you're considering a job (research, independent contracting, a two-person office, etcetera) that may keep you isolated from other employees.

Meaningful, Fulfilling Work

How important will it be at the end of the day for you to feel you've accomplished something? It could be closing a critical deal, helping people in need, or creating something lasting. What's meaningful or fulfilling to you isn't necessarily so for the next person.

Opportunity for Promotion

You should explore where the job will take you. What are the short-term and long-term possibilities? If it's responsibility, money, or management experience that you want, is there the potential to get it? Are there any requirements—work experience or a graduate degree, for example—that might prevent you from being promoted to where you'd like to be? Some of the best growth opportunities involve starting out at a lower level than you'd like; if the company has a policy of promoting from within, it might be well worth your while to put in your time as an entry-level employee. Make sure your expectations are realistic.

Opportunity to Innovate

Do you get the sense that this company encourages suggestions, new ideas, and efforts to improve systems? Or is it an organization that considers its policies tried and true? Are you an idea factory? Do you enjoy brainstorming, creating, or trying something untested? If so, you might be happiest in a job that provides you some freedom to create and be creative. If you prefer to pick up where innovators leave off, content to implement other people's ideas, that's a good thing to know about yourself.

Preparation for Graduate School

When you think about your long-term goals, is graduate school part of your future? If so, how will this opportunity transfer to your résumé? Certain career paths are well-tested conduits to business, law, or medical school; others prepare you better for graduate school in the arts, the sciences, or in education programs. Is it better to follow the normal path, or will you benefit from taking a riskier route? You need to decide which opportunity will provide you with the most relevant work experience and will help you tell the most compelling story. You should also consider a company's willingness to write recommendations or offer scholarship aid. If you have to apply to school without the knowledge of your supervisor, it will be tough to get a recommendation out of him.

Preparation for Other Fields

Are you looking for a way to launch your career? Jobs with broader descriptions or within expanding companies may expose you to a variety of work experiences. If you're looking to specialize, are you in a position to learn from a mentor or supervisor? The sooner you identify long-term career goals, the easier it is for you to evaluate a job's potential to help you along your path either within or outside of the company.

Professional Development

Now that you're ready to embark on a journey into the working world that will last longer than a summer or a semester, have you given much thought to what you wish to gain from the experience? Challenge, opportunity for promotion, and preparation for graduate school or other fields are all interrelated—they have to do with gaining skills, experience, and furthering your career. Are there skills you'd like to learn? Knowledge you'd like to gain? A goal you'd like to attain?

Responsibility and Autonomy

Are you happiest when you're given a project with which to run? Or do you prefer to be someone's right hand, following orders precisely, efficiently, and effectively? You may wish to pile all the responsibility you can gather onto your shoulders and be totally responsible for the results, or you may want to help other people who are in charge as you gradually ease into the world of accountability.

WHAT'S MISSING?

Is it realistic to expect a company to provide all of these benefits or to anticipate that your prospective employer is going to outline all of the possible rewards and details we just covered? Probably not. Don't read these lists and panic when you discover that you weren't offered tuition reimbursement or tempted by the incredible opportunity for growth at the company. Instead, try to familiarize yourself with the possibilities and identify what's most important to you. That way, you'll be able to look at the offer objectively and assess whether or not something of vital interest is missing.

A good strategy for making sure all of your questions are answered is to write them down ahead of time. Anything you're wondering about—from details on health care, the possible location of the job, or the uniform—should make this list. If you are given the chance to ask questions when the offer is extended, great. Ask away. If you aren't able to ask all of your questions or are sure that something else will pop into your head within two seconds of hanging up the phone or leaving the office, ask if it's all right to follow up with any remaining questions.

DON'T CAVE IN TO PRESSURE

Let's say you've test-driven a car and it drives like a dream. It has most of the options you hoped for, although you wanted a sun roof and did not need an automatic transmission. The salesperson is practically falling out of his chair in anticipation. He's discussing financing, licensing, payment information, and is ready to close the deal. What do you do? That's a great question, whether you're buying a car or accepting a job offer.

You do have some choices: You can agree to everything immediately, ask for time to think things over, or turn down the offer. Before you decide how you're going to act, consider one more thing. One fundamental difference between buying a car and taking a job is that while the salesman has what you want (a car), you have what the employer wants (you).

Some companies may give you an "exploding" offer, one in which your signing bonus (if there is one) is larger if you accept immediately, but goes down over time. Depending on the policies of your career center, these offers may be against the rules. You should never feel overly pressured to answer prematurely.

You've made it to the other side of the table. Now it's your turn to make a decision, and it's the company's turn to wait by the phone. If you need time, ask for it. Remember, though, that the company's timeline may be different from your own. Be clear about your needs, but also be prepared to be a little flexible, especially if you're serious about the company; that way, you'll add to an already favorable impression with your future employers. Don't abuse an employer's trust and ask for four months to decide, hoping that something better will come along. It's not fair to the company or to other applicants who might be eager for the opportunity.

. . . NOW WHAT?

Once the company decides that you should be its next new employee, you have become an investment, one that merits some attention. While companies will handle this differently, in some instances you'll be wined and dined, contacted by various employees eager to sing the company's praises, and encouraged to take every opportunity to glimpse how great life will be working with them. You may even be assigned to a company mentor, someone who will act as a resource.

It's a good idea to use these contacts to gather more data. Ask the probing questions you never had answered, observe how employees interact with each other, and inquire if it's possible to spend a day in the field, if that will help you make a decision. You might even have the chance to attend a company meeting, meet with your potential manager, or at least speak with some recent hires. Be reasonable—account for time, distance, and practicality, but don't be afraid to ask for what you need to make a good choice.

Now that you've considered all of the pieces of the offer, it's time to see how well it fits in with your needs as well as how it compares to other choices. In other words, it's time to weigh your options.

chapter 9
WEIGHING YOUR OPTIONS

Maybe your roommate from freshman year has always wanted to be in advertising. So much so that his enthusiasm bubbled over and when he applied, you applied. Oddly enough, you both got offers. You can continue to be great friends, work together, and maybe even find an apartment. A perfect scenario, right? Absolutely, if advertising is what you want to do. If it's not, you could end up in a work environment that may be perfectly right for him and terribly wrong for you. Many people accept offers in haste, only to discover that they aren't suited for the job they have taken. Before you think about what you want to do, take a minute to consider the kinds of situations you want to avoid.

COMMON REASONS FOR JOB DISSATISFACTION

The most common reasons for job dissatisfaction include:

Incorrectly Assessing Interests/Aptitudes

You may have developed excellent, specific skills; whether or not you enjoy using them on a daily basis is another matter. If you are skilled at number crunching but find it boring, that accounting job will drive you nuts.

Doing Work That's Not Challenging or Interesting Enough

Some jobs have you start out learning the basics before being promoted. Make sure you're prepared for entry-level work, if you're set on the long-term goal.

Following Your Parents' Dreams, Not Your Own

Just because your whole family went into engineering is no reason to assume that your destiny lies in that direction. It's not easy to separate your wishes from those of your parents, but you'll have to try.

Going for the Money

Making money hand over fist isn't always enough. You're the only one who knows how important a high salary is, relative to the value of the work you do.

Losing Sight of the Bottom Line

Even if you've got the best job ever, it won't do you much good if you have to live in your office because you can't afford an apartment.

Going With the Flow, Not With Your Heart

Don't go into Teach for America because everyone else is; go into it because you want to teach.

Doing the "Sensible Thing"

Don't choose a career path merely because somewhere along the way you picked up the idea that it "makes sense" for someone of your background. Sense to whom? The sum total of you is made up of a lot more than your background.

WHERE DO YOU WANT TO GO?

Now it's time to step back from the job offer and the interview process for a moment and think about where you want to go. Not where you'll be tomorrow night, after commencement, or even this summer, but where you want to go in a year, in five years, in a lifetime. To make the best decision possible on your offer, you'll need to be honest with yourself about what you hope to accomplish within and outside of your career.

You must have given this some thought when you were researching employers, writing your résumé, and preparing for interviews. You might even have discovered that you have two sets of goals, one that you tell people about because you think it's what they want to hear, and one that you keep to yourself because you're not so sure it's reachable. Revisit your goals now. You're not trying to impress an interviewer, placate your parents, or fit in with your friends. This is just about you—your dreams, your aspirations, your life. If you're the kind of person who needs to work things out on paper, the following exercise might be helpful. Make a list of the following goals.

Personal Goals:
- Interests I've enjoyed pursuing
- Interests I'd like to explore further
- Skills I'd like to use in life
- Something I'm passionate about
- In one year, I'd like to be . . .
- In five years, I'd like to be . . .
- Forgetting about what's possible or not, one thing that I'd love to do with my life if I could

Professional Goals:
- Interests in which I've developed a decent level of skill
- Skills I'd like to explore further
- Skills I'd like to use in my career
- Something I'm passionate about
- In one year, I'd like to be . . .
- In five years, I'd like to be . . .
- Forgetting about what's possible or not, one thing that I'd love to do with my life if I could

Goals are not set in stone. As you develop professional skills, experience, and interests, your responses to these questions will shift accordingly. You don't need to draw a map full of every little detail and road sign; as long as you sense the general direction and make note of the most important land marks, you should have enough to guide you in filling out the table below and coming to a decision about your offer.

WEIGHING YOUR OPTIONS

Whether you're considering one offer or ten, you'll need to understand which factors are most critical for you, how well a company's offer matches your needs, and what you're going to do about it. The following chart should help you with the first two steps.

How to Use the Chart:

1) Take another look at the lists of potential benefits and rewards discussed in chapter 8.
2) Rank them on a scale of 1–13 in order of importance to you.
3) Fill in the "Company Names" section with companies that have extended you offers.
4) Compare your needs with what has been offered.

REWARDS	RANK	COMPANY NAMES		
CHALLENGE				
COMMUNITY INVOLVEMENT				
COMPENSATION & BENEFITS				
COMPANY CULTURE & MISSION				
FUN				
GREAT COLLEAGUES				
MEANINGFUL, FULFILLING WORK				
OPPORTUNITY FOR PROMOTION				
OPPORTUNITY TO INNOVATE				
PREPARATION FOR GRAD SCHOOL				
PREPARATION FOR OTHER FIELDS				
PROFESSIONAL DEVELOPMENT				
RESPONSIBILITY & AUTONOMY				

Once you've ranked these areas according to your requirements and have evaluated how the offer(s) you're considering compare, you should have a better idea of where the two diverge. If you're considering multiple offers, go ahead and rank each offer separately.

To illustrate how this process works, let's take a look at an example that assumes that you've received an offer from Acme Corporation. It might make things clearer if we rank your list and Acme Corp.'s list side by side.

Your Preferences	Acme Corp.'s Rankings
1. Preparation for grad school	1. Challenge
2. Compensation & benefits	2. Responsibility & autonomy
3. Responsibility & autonomy	3. Great colleagues
4. Great colleagues	4. Preparation for grad school
5. Opportunity for promotion	5. Fun
6. Challenge	6. Professional development
7. Fun	7. Compensation & benefits
8. Company culture & mission	8. Opportunity for promotion
9. Meaningful, fulfilling work	9. Preparation for other fields
10. Opportunity to innovate	10. Meaningful, fulfilling work
11. Professional development	11. Company culture & mission
12. Community involvement	12. Opportunity to innovate
13. Preparation for other fields	13. Community involvement

To identify potential problem areas, let's make a list of the factors that were three or more rankings apart. In this example, that gives us:

- Compensation & benefits (your list, 2; the company, 7)
- Challenge (your list, 6; the company, 1)
- Professional development (your list, 11; the company, 6)
- Preparation for other fields (your list, 13; the company, 9)

Out of this group, compensation and benefits is the only consideration that ranked lower on the list of the company's ratings than on your list of requirements. Challenge, opportunity for professional development, and preparation for other fields all ranked higher for this company than you were necessarily looking for. When comparing your needs with those of the company, it would appear that this company will offer a greater challenge and less compensation than you had in mind. You will obviously have to do some serious thinking about how hard you are willing to work, and how little compensation you are prepared to accept, before you make a decision on this offer.

APPROACHING A DECISION

Now that you've taken a moment to consider where you'd like to go and where a job might take you, it's time to put everything together. If you've ranked your requirements for a job, reviewed any offer(s) you've been given, and considered how these meet your needs, you should be close to a decision. You just might have an obvious answer to the question of what you should do. If so, you're lucky. A more likely scenario is that you are looking at an option that's almost right. If it only did this or gave you that, then you would be happy. If so, it's probably time to negotiate.

chapter 10
NEGOTIATING

Your dream job—the one that meets all of your needs, whether that includes letting you work with incredible colleagues, giving you as much responsibility and challenge as you desire, paying you extremely well, providing you with a direct career path to your long-term goal, or putting you in a position to do fulfilling work that helps you and others—probably doesn't exist anywhere but in your dreams. Realistically, you may need to compromise and settle for an opportunity that meets most of them. If you can get a job that fulfills 75 percent of your requirements, would that satisfy you? You have a choice. Accept the offer as is and be happy with your decision, or try to make some changes. How willing are you to haggle over the other 25 percent?

POINTS TO CONSIDER

Before you approach the company with your demands, it's a good idea to determine what might be negotiable and what is most likely set in stone. Your odds of getting what you ask for increase if you do some homework.

Some Possible Shortcomings in an Offer:

- Commute or location is less than ideal
- Culture or office climate doesn't quite suit you
- Job description includes tasks you don't like or excludes those you do
- Offer is for a finite period (an internship or one year stay)
- Policies are unclear
- Position is more entry-level than you'd expected
- Salary is lower than you'd like

- Schedule is too demanding or unconventional
- Start date is too soon or too far off for your tastes
- Vacation plan doesn't work with prior commitments
- Work doesn't hold any meaning for you

How negotiable are these points? It depends on the company, of course. Here are some general guidelines for you to work from:

Commute

This may be negotiable. How far you must travel to get to work is pretty closely tied to where you will be living and where you'd like to work. If you've been offered a position with a predetermined location, one that doesn't work well for you, you may be out of luck. If, however, you haven't been assigned to an office yet, you should definitely make any preferences that you have known. Remember that flexibility is a nice quality in an employee. Also, you might be able to arrange for a slightly different schedule to allow you to arrive before or after peak commuting hours. Some companies will even allow you to work out of your home every once in a while. That's not a realistic possibility for some positions. If your acceptance or refusal depends on the commute alone, you should mention your problem.

Culture

This is non-negotiable. There's not much you can do about a culture or office climate that you don't like. The chances of the company changing to fit your personality or work style are slim to none (unless it's a one-person office). You need to decide if this is a big enough hurdle to prevent you from accepting the job.

Job Description

If you are filling a role that has been the same at the company for years, there won't be much room for changes. If, however, your company is fast-growth and always looking for the chance to give an employee more responsibility, you may have quite a bit of room in which to change your responsibilities. You can always express your concern or interest to the company and ask how likely it will be that you'll be able to do some work for the marketing department, for example. You should also think about where the job might take you within the company and whether or not that position meets your needs better.

Finite Offer

If your offer is for a finite period, you have very little room in which to negotiate. If you accept the offer, you'll have to do so for the time period they've indicated. Rather than negotiate this point, consider the value of the experience and whether or not you can reapply for another position at the company. While there's no guarantee that you'll be offered a permanent position at the end of your assignment, expressing an interest won't hurt.

Policies

These are also most likely non-negotiable. The best thing to do if you're unsure of a policy is to ask to see a copy of the employee handbook, a summary of health care or other benefits, vacation, expense reimbursement, or business travel to review the policy in question. If you have concerns, you can certainly express them, but don't expect the company to change something just because of you.

Entry-Level Position

This is similar to considering an opportunity that has an unsatisfactory job description. While you can't negotiate for a higher-level position, you can ask about opportunities for advancement. You can express your strong interest in working on special projects and developing yourself by contributing to the company's needs. Emphasize that you'll work hard to get ahead; don't approach it with a "What can you do for me?" kind of attitude. That probably won't get you very far.

127

Salary

Salary is also difficult to negotiate. Even if a company wants you enough to offer you more money or at least a signing bonus, these costs may not be within its budget. If you have received other offers that will pay you more, you might be in a slightly better position to ask for more money, but don't count on it. It would be different if you had years of experience and really stood out from the field of applicants. In this case, you are competing with a number of other college-educated but experience-poor applicants who might take the job at the offered salary and be grateful.

Schedule

This depends on the company and the nature of the work. If it's essential that all employees be at work at the same time, you won't be able to change your schedule. If you need an evening off now and again because of a class you want to take, find out if it's possible to come in early or on weekends to make up time.

Start Date

Some companies require you to complete a formal training program and may have arranged your start date around such training. Others may have an urgent need for new hires to begin as soon as possible during the summer, or would prefer that they start late in the fall. You won't know unless you ask. Your reasons for putting off a start date should be better than wanting to relax at the beach all summer. This is worth asking about.

Time Off

Time off is negotiable (within reason). If you'd already planned a vacation that will conflict with your start date or would require you to take time off right after you've begun, be honest. This is the best time for you to request time off. The company still wants something from you (your acceptance of the offer), and will make an effort to accommodate you if they can, although it may be in the form of an unpaid leave rather than paid vacation.

There may be other factors that are more important to you than the ones listed above. You'll have to identify those and think about the likelihood of gaining some ground on your own.

RESEARCH

There's one more thing you should do before approaching the company with questions or demands. Remember the categories you looked into when you were researching the company prior to the interview? You came up with information and questions regarding the job, the company, and the industry. Research may help you decide if your demands are within reason, especially if you have concerns regarding job responsibilities, standard compensation, or industry outlook. Your best resources are company employees or your career center's library.

Employees

You might want to shadow an employee for a day, attend a staff meeting, or talk to someone so you can ask any lingering questions. If you haven't had time to do so, we'd recommend it. You won't get a lot of sensitive information this way, but you might gain a feel for the job above and beyond the description printed on a page.

> **Don't Miss This Resource**
>
> An excellent resource to start with is the *Occupational Outlook Handbook*. It is published by the U.S. Department of Labor's Bureau of Labor Statistics and provides detailed information on a wide array of occupations, including industry outlook, training, job descriptions, salary ranges, and lists of resources. The handbook is a bit dry, but chock full of helpful information. If your career center doesn't have a copy, it is available online (at http://stats.bls.gov/ocohome.htm).

Career Center Library

If you're curious to know more about the specifics of a job or the industry in general, revisit your career center library. Your career center may also be a source of typical salary ranges for recent alumni or more advice on negotiating an offer.

ASKING QUESTIONS, MAKING DEMANDS

Get a piece of paper and write down what you wish to cover in the conversation. Which points will you need to learn more about, which will you need to clarify, and what's the next step? You should have a contact name, either from your initial interviews or from the meeting when you were offered the job.

Try to convey the impression of someone who's seriously considering an offer, has intelligent questions to ask, and is thorough. You don't want to appear overly aggressive, anxious, or insensitive. That may be the difference between making demands and asking questions. Remember that this could be your boss; try to conduct a conversation that will help rather than hinder your future relationship with the representative and the company.

Some Things to Keep in Mind When You're Negotiating:

- Be polite. Remember to greet the company representative with assurance, and thank him for his time.
- Identify yourself: Remind him of who you are and why you are calling.
- Ask if it's a good time to discuss details of the offer.
- Be prepared to schedule an appointment if necessary.
- Mention that you appreciate the offer and think it's an exciting opportunity before bringing up your questions.
- It's not a bad idea to begin with one or two points in the offer that you like.
- You might summarize your concerns briefly and gauge the reaction before going into greater detail.
- Once you've tested the waters, decide on which points to elaborate, and remember that you should try to include alternative suggestions.
- Give an ultimatum or threat only if you're really prepared to act on it.
- It's possible that the company representative will need to think about what you've said before giving you an answer. If so, let him know when he can reach you and set a deadline.
- Arrange for the next step in the process (either agree to send in your response by the required date, or arrange a follow-up conversation if necessary).
- Reiterate your interest in the company and thank him for his time.

MAKING CONCESSIONS

You've got your list of things you absolutely must have. Then there are those points that, while important, aren't deal makers or breakers. Now that you have all of the facts, you may need to choose between looking for another job or taking one that's not entirely what you want.

Certain points that seemed absolutely essential to you earlier in the process may now seem like concessions you might be willing to make if it makes the difference between working or not. If, for example, you find that you'll need to give up your ideal start date and begin working two months earlier than originally planned, why not try to bargain a little? Explain that you'll start when they need you, but ask if they would be willing to move you to a location that's closer to what you'd originally requested.

Think very carefully about saying no to a job that meets most of your needs, especially if you feel that changes might be made once you've been there for a little while. You might even rethink when you're available to begin working, where you're willing to work, or how much you'll get paid if the rest of the offer meets your needs.

MAKING A DECISION

No one will decide this for you; only you can do that. If you've already tried the lists described in chapter 10 and you're tired of being rational, objective, and methodical, why not put all of the names in a hat and pull one out? This may sound a bit simplistic, but it's actually not a bad exercise. If you pull out a name and your first response is one of irritation, displeasure, or disappointment, this company is probably wrong for you. If, on the other hand, you

You've Done This Before . . .

This isn't the first time you've had to make a momentous decision. Remember selecting a college? Did you visit the schools, read all of the literature, and grill alums and enrolled students? You probably went through the motions of making an "educated" decision before going with your gut. Choosing a job is similar. Ultimately, you're likely to go with the one that "feels right."

feel like a weight has been lifted, or filled with anticipation, then you've probably made the right choice.

This hat exercise is a useful way of identifying some of the underlying emotions at work here. No matter how rationally you approach this decision, there is no getting away from the fact that emotions are involved. You're not just choosing a job—you're choosing a path that will take you beyond school.

People react to change in different ways. You may be a nervous wreck when you contemplate the future, or you might be filled with excitement and anticipation about the next step. Either way, you're going to make a choice that will affect you for some time. If you're balking at making a decision, look at the reasons that are holding you back and make sure they're valid. There are objections to a particular job and then there are objections to jobs in general. While it's good to be aware of your preferences regarding attire, schedules, work load, and so forth, you shouldn't reject an offer just because you need to wear a suit, get to work by 8, and actually agree to be there five days a week, day after day. We mention this not to make you take any job that's offered to you, but to encourage you to be realistic about your negotiating points.

Also keep in mind that people love to give advice about jobs. Family, friends, acquaintances: Everyone has an opinion. With so much input readily available, you may feel even more pressure than you're putting on yourself (admit it—you're sick of the "and what will you be doing after school?" question). Never lose sight of the fact that ultimately, your decision is about you. If you do, you may find that you choose a job for the wrong reasons.

chapter 11
TIME TO CELEBRATE

The champagne is chilling, your offer letter is posted on your door, and you've changed your answering machine from your professional voice to festive, celebratory music. Now that you're part of that group known as the gainfully employed, you're even feeling magnanimous enough to provide champagne for your roommates. They'll need it, since they have yet to find a job. Life, in short, looks pretty darn good right about now. Right? Absolutely. But don't forget to wrap up a few details.

FINALIZING THE OFFER

You've decided to accept an offer. You know it, your family knows it, and it's a good bet that most of your immediate acquaintance knows it as well. But what about the company? Take a look at the offer letter. It just might include a brief description of the job you've been offered, a summary of salary and other benefits, a mention of start dates, and even a space where you're supposed to sign your name before returning the letter to the company. Amidst all of the excitement and mayhem of senior year, don't forget to return this! You should also make a copy for your records.

If you didn't receive an offer letter or any other kind of contract or agreement to sign, you might want to write an acceptance letter in which you summarize your understanding of the offer including job title, start dates, and if you feel so inclined, a salary range. You should sign this, make a copy, and send it to the company. If you're still not satisfied that everything is final, call and ask if there's anything else you need to supply them with or if you should just wait to hear regarding training and your first day.

GETTING A BETTER OFFER

Once you've signed an offer letter or letter of intent to work for the company, it's probably safe to assume that everything is settled. But what do you do when you hear from that long-shot opportunity you applied for on a whim, the job you really wanted but were sure you wouldn't get? On the one hand, you've given your word, and you may feel obliged to honor it. On the other hand, one could argue that it's your life, and your decision; you could just decide to go with the company that offers you the best choice.

Changing Your Mind

If you decide to change your mind after accepting an offer, you won't be the first to do so. According to a recent *New York Times* article focusing mainly on MBA recruiting, a growing number of students are reneging on job offers. A decade ago, this was rare; now, recruiters estimate that one or two students among every 10 who sign job-commitment letters will send a letter before the start date saying she will be doing something else.

We can't tell you which choice to make. However, if you do decide to go with the better offer, there are certain things you really should do. First of all, the sooner you let the people who hired you know, the better. They'll be disappointed, perhaps even angry. But they'll need as much time as possible to find a replacement. Don't cop out and send a brief letter, leave a short voicemail, or an impersonal e-mail. The company put time and effort into finding you and treating you with respect; you should reciprocate. You don't need to deliver the bad news in person, but at least make sure you have a conversation with someone.

If you can, be honest. Did it come down to a position of greater responsibility, opportunity, or compensation? If so, say so. The company may appreciate hearing how their offer measures up to others. Finally, keep the interaction as professional, courteous, and sincere as you can. Depending on how well you handle this, you may even leave behind you an open door that would otherwise have been firmly shut.

TYING UP LOOSE ENDS

Now that it's a done deal, you're just about ready to close the book on your job search. Before you do that, here's a quick rundown of details to keep in mind.

Your Address

Once you've officially accepted the offer, make sure you leave the recruiter with an address that will be good after you leave school. Companies often want to send you new employee packets or other information (including training materials, tax forms, applications, etcetera). Try not to drop off the face of the earth. If the company doesn't know how to reach you, it might not be able to include you in the training group as planned.

Employer References

You may need proof of employment to help with apartment leases or car loans. Ask your contact at the company if he or she is willing to verify your employment or if someone else in the office can do so.

Health Insurance

You should ask about when health insurance begins. Some companies have enrollment periods, which means that you may have a window of a month or two during which you'll need to arrange for other coverage.

Prior Commitments or Obligations

If you're going to require time off in excess of what the company allows, or if you'll need to use vacation days before you've earned them, say so before you get started! Companies don't like surprises, and may not be able to grant you what you need once you begin working. If you tell them ahead of time, you'll have a better chance of getting what you want.

Referral Bonuses

Some companies offer bonuses to employees whose referrals are hired. In addition, companies sometimes like help in publicizing campus recruiting activities. If you're interested, find out whether or not you'll have the chance to participate in recruiting on campus.

Start Date and Other Arrangements

You'll want to set an official start date. Find out exactly where you should be, at what time, what to expect, what to bring, and what to wear (you can always request information on uniforms or dress codes if you're not sure). Your start date may be far enough in the future to merit waiting on these arrangements. If so, make sure that you have a contact name and number. That way, you can ask about when you'll hear from the company regarding your start date, and you'll be able to keep an eye on the mail or expect a phone call.

Thanking Those Who Helped

Finding a job is sometimes a group effort, requiring assistance, patience, advice, and sympathy from friends, family, professors, and former employers. Once you've concluded your search, you should go back and thank those who helped you. It's the polite thing to do, obviously. It also makes sense. Building a professional network takes time. Because you never know when you'll be looking for your next job or helping friends make their own inquiries, it's the smart thing as well.

And now, don't you have classes to get to, papers to write, champagne to drink, books to hunt down, and a life to live? It's time to celebrate and enjoy the remainder of your time in college. Congratulations! You've earned it.

section **4**

APPENDIX

APPENDIX

BOOKS

As you probably know from your trips to the career center, the library, or the bookstore, there is no shortage of career-related books. Here's a short list of books covering everything from assessing what you want to do to recent graduates' experiences out in the working world.

Careers for Culture Lovers & Other Artsy Types, published by VGM Career Horizons, is one example of a book series that targets people whose interests may seem unconventional and who aren't sure how to find a satisfying career. Other titles include *Careers for People Who Love to Write*, . . . *Who Love Animals*, and . . .*Who Love Sports*.

Doing What You Love, Loving What You Do, by Dr. Robert Anthony. Published by Berkeley Publishing Group. Copyright 1991.

First Job, Great Job: America's Hottest Business Leaders Share their Secrets, by Jason R. Rich. Published by Macmillan Spectrum, USA. 1996. *First Job. . .* contains interviews with some well known presidents and CEOs of such companies as Yahoo! and Mrs. Fields. Rich's goal is to provide soon-to-be- graduates with guidance and advice to help them make informed decisions.

Going Indie: Self Employment, Freelance & Temping Opportunities, by Kathi Elster and Katherine Crowley. Published by Kaplan Educational Centers and Simon & Schuster. The purpose of this book is to help you identify the best self-employment option for you. Includes interviews with people who have been there and have successfully embarked on their own.

The Hidden Job Market (Princeton, NJ: Peterson's Guides). This book provides listings by state, company, city, and industry of fast-growing high tech companies.

The Job Seekers' Guide to Socially Responsible Companies (Gale Research, Inc., Detroit, MI. 1995). Edited by Katherine Jankowski. This guide includes company profiles, contact info, and geographic and location indices for 1,000+ companies.

The Seven Habits of Highly Effective People, by Stephen Covey. Seven habits that will make it easier for you to achieve your personal and professional goals.

So . . . What Are You Doing After College? Real-Life Advice from People Who've Been There. Edited by Sven Newman. Published by Owl Books, Henry Holt and Co., New York. A collection of frank, informative essays that include practical, helpful tips for getting your foot in the door in a variety of fields.

Standard & Poor's Register of Corporations, Directors, and Executives. Published annually by Standard & Poor. In three volumes. A good source for researching larger corporations.

What Color is Your Parachute?, by Richard Nelson Bolles, is absolutely crammed with helpful resources. A series of exercises culminate in creating your ideal job map. Printed annually.

ONLINE RESOURCES

Most college students have internet and world wide web access through their dorms, through computer rooms on campus, or at the library. You may also be able to access the web at your career center.

While it's fun to surf, keep in mind that you're doing so for a purpose. If you find that you are too easily distracted and keep ending up at Letterman's top ten list or checking in on chat rooms, you may need to put yourself on an electronic leash. Find a friend—perhaps someone else who is going through a similar search—and keep each other honest. You don't want to waste valuable time that you should be devoting to your job search.

If you have access to it, Netscape is one of the best tools. It automatically hooks you up to Yahoo! and Alta Vista, two directories that are user-friendly and well organized.

Here's a list of some internet sites that may prove helpful. They run the gamut, from an online bookstore to job sites designed specifically for the soon-to-be college graduate. The amount of information that's available online is growing exponentially and is already overwhelming. Your best strategy may be to focus on a few sites rather than sampling a wide range.

Academic Employment Network
http://www.academploy.com
A site that offers information on educational opportunities, including faculty, staff, and administrator positions at both public and private schools, as well as some private sector jobs.

Amazon.Com
http://www.amazon.com
Self-described as "Earth's Biggest Bookstore," this is an excellent resource if you're trying to track down books. You can order books as you browse listings (they even give you an electronic shopping cart!).

Australia's Careers Online Virtual Careers Show
http://www.careersonline.com.au/show/menu.html
This site is a "virtual career show" in that you can choose an interest area, view the occupations listed in that category, select one, and read a detailed description of the nature of the work, training, job outlook, earnings, related occupations, and sources of additional information.

The Best Jobs in the USA Today
http://www.bestjobsusa.com/
This site features jobs which have been posted in the *USA Today* as well

as some additional listings. The site features a free résumé depository, a career store, and a national career events calendar. You can search by category, title, or state. The listings are updated every 48 hours.

The Boston Job Bank
http://www.bostonjobs.com
Depending on where you wish to work after graduation, you may want to check out some of the more regional sites. The Boston Job Bank is one possibility.

BridgePath Employment Services
http://www.bridgepath.com
This sight is specifically geared to students, and offers automatic internship notification, online job-related chat rooms, and job listings.

Career Magazine
http://www.careermag.com
This site is comprehensive, easily navigable, and has great articles. According to Emory University's "List of Colossal Career Links" and the Riley Guide, the Career Magazine is one of the premiere "massive career search services."

The Career Mart
http://www.careermart.com
Here you can search on college campuses for campus interviews and career center information. It also has sections on high-tech opportunities, market research, employment advice, and career fair info.

Career Mosaic
http://www.careermosaic.com
This site holds a lot of information. While you cannot browse by employer or location, the search engine is particularly strong, allowing you to search the J.O.B.S. database by almost any criteria. In addition to the jobs database, there is a top usenet group posting feature, a career resource center, guides to the job search, help on résumé writing, and a college connection featuring companies that actively recruit college graduates.

Career Path

http://www.careerpath.com.

You can view classified ads online at this site.

Career Resource Center

http://www.careers.org

This is a comprehensive source of information for the job-seeker, including a very helpful list of sites you should visit.

College Grad Job Hunter

http://www.collegegrad.com

This site gives soon-to-be or recent college graduates pointers on the whole job-seeking process, from figuring out what it is they want to do to negotiating job offers. The site is very easy to use.

College Recruiter Magazine

http://www.college-recruiter.com

Specifically geared toward college students who are looking for full-time and part-time positions, this site includes links to company websites, automatic résumé submission, links to articles, and a section for high school students searching for a job.

Entry-Level Job Seeker Assistant

http://members.aol.com/Dylander/jobhome.html

A site that is dedicated to helping the candidate with less than a year's work experience or no formal experience to find an entry-level job.

The Good Works

http://www.essential.org/goodworks

A site designed for those of you looking for socially responsible jobs. It provides computer networking to over 300 industry professionals and over 30 non-profit organizations.

Hoffman Recruiters

http://www.hoffmanrecruiters.com

An interesting site that includes a detailed sign-up sheet for half-hour first round interviews. If you make the first cut, the site will refer you to companies for free. These companies range from consulting, accounting, and investment banking to software, biotech, and internet companies.

Job Bank USA
http://www.jobbankusa.com
Linked to Career Mosaic and Career Magazine. You can search job listings by key words and post your résumé online.

Job Direct
http://www.jobdirect.com
This site's student zone will take you through registration, putting together an online résumé, and posting your résumé online, and will also let you browse through job listings.

Job Hunt
http://www.job-hunt.org
A "Meta-list of OnLine Job-Search Resources and Services," this site is a great jumping-off point for different job listings and other resources for finding a job.

JobMarket
http://www.thejobmarket.com
The site includes company profiles, classifieds, and a section on résumé building, job fair calendar, and an advice forum.

Job Smart, the California Job Search Guide
http://www.jobsmarts.com
A site with a heavy California focus, Jobsmart offers job listings, help with résumé writing, a career guide, salary info, a section on the hidden job market, and a chance to "Ask Electra," the personal online librarian.

JobSource
http://www.jobsource.com
Another site geared toward students who are searching for entry-level, part-time, or full-time opportunities or internships. Includes links to company web pages as well as chat rooms in which to seek advice.

Jobtrak

http://www.jobtrak.com

This is *the* site for job listings. Jobtrak was probably the first online job listing resource. Early on, they made a deal with most college career centers to give a share of their profits back to them in exchange for direct access to college students served by the centers. You will probably be able to access this directly from your career center.

Job Web

http://www.jobweb.com

This official website of NACE (the National Association of Colleges and Employers) is an excellent resource for the college student. The site features "The Catapult," NACE's meta list and resource guide, which has a great links page of U.S. and international resources.

Kaplan Educational Centers

http://www.kaplan.com

This web site includes a section called "Test Yourself" that may be helpful for career assessment. Kaplan also has a classified ads section as well as a helpful resource list. Here are the direct addresses:

> Kaplan's Career Center: http://www.kaplan.com/career/
> Kaplan Career Library:
> http://www.kaplan.com/library/career/.html#classifieds

Monster Board

http://www.monster.com

In addition to a cool theme song, the Monster Board offers a great search engine and résumé posting. It tends to list primarily Californian and northeastern jobs.

The Nation's Job Search

http://www.nationjob.com/education

This site lists job in education. You have the option of using a free "search scout" that will E-mail more specific listings matching your preferences to you.

Occupational Outlook Handbook

http://stats.bls.gov/ocohome.htm

This handbook, published by the U.S. Department of Labor's Bureau of Labor Statistics, provides detailed information on occupations, including industry outlook, training, job descriptions, salary ranges, and lists of resources to check out for more information.

Online Career Center

http://www.occ.com

Again, a site that includes resources in addition to job listings. It features a résumé database to which you can add your résumé; this is accessible to employers searching the database by keyword.

The Riley Guide

http://www.dbm.com/jobguide/careers.html

A comprehensive guide to the flood of online resources. It not only gives you a good rundown of what's around, it provides links to web sites.

The Student Center

http://www.studentcenter.com

This is more of an online guidance center and a link to other sites than a place to find job listings. It is targeted to college, graduate, and recent graduate students.

The Virtual Job Fair

http://www.careerexpo.com

This site focuses on technology-related jobs and has a tech career resource feature, a high tech career magazine, and close to 15,000 high tech opportunities (located in Silicon Valley).

Wet Feet Press

http://www.wetfeet.com/webc/wetfeet/home.html

"The Information Service for Job Seekers," Wet Feet Press provides insider reports on companies. This is a way to order reports on companies before interviewing with them.

What Color is Your Parachute: Job Hunting Online
http://www.washingtonpost.com/parachute
An online guide to online career hunting. Richard Bolles' helpful approach to locating a job now has another section that focuses on using the internet to your best advantage.

Yahoo! Employment Classifieds
http://www.classifieds.yahoo.com/employment.html
You can search the job listings by keywords, metro regions, or by states. You can also browse the listings nationwide. While the search engine is easily used, many of these jobs may require some work experience in the field.

CAREER CENTER RESOURCES

Ideally, your school's career center will provide you with what you need. If not, or if you'd like to get a second opinion, the following college career center websites seem to stand out from the rest. If you're having difficulties finding opportunities from where you are, we'd encourage you to explore the websites of any schools that are close to where you're planning on settling.

Internet Sites for Job Seekers and Employers
http://www.ups.purdue.edu/student/jobsites.htm

Northwestern University Career Services
http://www.stuaff.nwu.edu/ucs

University of Massachusetts/Amherst
http://www.umassp.edu/html/career/student_toc.html

Georgetown University's Career Education Center
http://careerweb.georgetown.edu/main3html

University of Virginia's Office of Career Planning & Placement
http://minerva.acc.Virginia.EDU/~career/menu.html

Harvard Business School, Baker Library: Career Resource Guides
http://www.library.hbs.edu/jobguide.htm

Exploring Occupations: Getting You Started on Your Career Path!
http://www.umanitoba.ca/student/counselling/crc.html

Career Paradise
http://www.emory.edu/CAREER/

Business Job Finder
http://www.cob.ohio-state.edu/dept/fin/osujobs.htm

About

KAPLAN

Educational Centers

K aplan Educational Centers is one of the nation's premier education companies, providing individuals with a full range of resources to achieve their educational and career goals. Kaplan, celebrating its 60th anniversary, is a wholly-owned subsidiary of The Washington Post Company.

TEST PREPARATION & ADMISSIONS

Kaplan's nationally-recognized test prep courses cover more than 20 standardized tests, including entrance exams for secondary school, college, and graduate school as well as foreign language and professional licensing exams. In addition, Kaplan offers private tutoring and comprehensive, one-to-one admissions and application advice for students applying to graduate school.

SCORE! EDUCATIONAL CENTERS

SCORE! after-school learning centers help students in grades K-8 build academic skills, confidence, and goal-setting skills in a motivating, sports-oriented environment. Kids use a cutting-edge, interactive curriculum that continually assesses and adapts to their academic needs and learning style. Enthusiastic Academic Coaches serve as positive role models, creating a high-energy atmosphere where learning is exciting and fun for kids. With nearly 40 centers today, SCORE! continues to open new centers nationwide.

KAPLAN LEARNING SERVICES

Kaplan Learning Services provides customized assessment, education, and training programs to K-12 schools, universities, and businesses to help students and employees reach their educational and career goals.

KAPLAN INTERNATIONAL

Kaplan serves international students and professionals in the U.S. through Access America, a series of intensive English language programs, and LCP International Institute, a leading provider of intensive English language programs at on-campus centers in California, Washington, and New York. Kaplan and LCP offer specialized services to sponsors including placement at top American universities, fellowship management, academic monitoring and reporting, and financial administration.

KAPLOAN

Students can get key information and advice about educational loans for college and graduate school through **KapLoan** (Kaplan Student Loan Information Program). Through an affiliation with one of the nation's largest student loan providers, **KapLoan** helps direct students and their families through the often bewildering financial aid process.

KAPLAN PUBLISHING

Kaplan Books, a joint imprint with Simon & Schuster, publishes books in test preparation, admissions, education, career development and life skills; Kaplan and *Newsweek* jointly publish the highly successful guides, **How to Get Into College** and **How to Choose a Career & Graduate School**. *SCORE!* and *Newsweek* have teamed up to publish **How to Help Your Child Suceed in School**.

Kaplan InterActive delivers award-winning, high quality educational products and services including Kaplan's best-selling **Higher Score** test-prep software and sites on the internet (http://www.kaplan.com) and America Online. Kaplan and Cendant Software are jointly developing, marketing and distributing educational software for the kindergarten through twelfth grade retail and school markets.

KAPLAN CAREER SERVICES

Kaplan helps students and graduates find jobs through Kaplan Career Services, the leading provider of career fairs in North America. The division includes **Crimson & Brown Associates**, the nation's leading diversity recruiting and publishing firm, and **The Lendman Group and Career Expo**, both of which help clients identify highly sought-after technical personnel and sales and marketing professionals.

COMMUNITY OUTREACH

Kaplan provides educational resources to thousands of financially disadvantaged students annually, working closely with educational institutions, not-for-profit groups, government agencies and other grass roots organizations on a variety of national and local support programs. Also, Kaplan centers enrich local communities by employing high school, college and graduate students, creating valuable work experiences for vast numbers of young people each year.

Want more information about our services, products, or the nearest Kaplan center?

Call our nationwide toll-free numbers:

1-800-KAP-TEST for information on our live courses, private tutoring and admissions consulting
1-800-KAP-ITEM for information on our products
1-888-KAP-LOAN* for information on student loans

Connect with us in cyberspace:

On AOL, keyword:"Kaplan"
On the World Wide Web, go to: http://www.kaplan.com
Via e-mail: info@kaplan.com

Write to:

Kaplan Educational Centers
888 Seventh Avenue
New York, NY 10106

Kaplan is a registered trademark of Kaplan Educational Centers. All rights reserved. *Kaplan is not a lender and does not participate in determinations of loan eligibility.